★

AMERICAN
VIGNETTES

★

AMERICAN VIGNETTES

A Collection of Footnotes to History

John I. White

Original Drawings by Jerry Allison

TravelVision®
A Division of General Drafting Co., Inc.
Convent Station, New Jersey

© 1976 by *TravelVision*®

CONTENTS

PREFACE

One turns to conventional history books for the broad picture of our country's first 200 years—its expansion across a continent, the wars it has fought, the political, social and economic changes that have taken place. *American Vignettes,* as the subtitle states, is largely a collection of footnotes to this overall view of our development.

With rare exceptions, the events chronicled on the following pages did not change the course of history. Yet they contributed to the interesting life of a growing and changing nation. Some stories deal with well known personalities, others with characters whose fame was short-lived. Benjamin Franklin, Abraham Lincoln and Henry Ford have their chapters. So do comparative unknowns such as feminist Amelia Bloomer, telephone pioneer Almon B. Strowger, and Perry McDonough Collins who dreamed of linking San Francisco and European Russia by telegraph via the Bering Strait.

Certain of the stories probably will surprise you. Did you know that the Southwest once experienced an ostrich-farming boom? Or that of necessity many thousands of homesteaders on the treeless prairies built their houses of sod and burned twisted hanks of hay in their stoves?

Other chapters may tickle your funnybone, like the hassle that ensued when a minor Treasury official had his own likeness printed on a 5-cent note. Or Franklin D. Roosevelt's disturbing pronouncement that Thanksgiving was too close to Christmas.

You may even wonder about the state of the business community when you read how some of its prominent members were taken in by smooth-talking confidence men.

The events and personages described here were all part of the ever-changing scene in a nation that found so much room for expansion and offered so many opportunities.

—John I. White

TRAVELS OF A ROLL OF PARCHMENT

If famous pieces of inscribed parchment were able to tell about their circuitous travels, few could spin a stranger tale than the faded document headed "The unanimous Declaration of the thirteen united States of America" which now resides in the National Archives Building in Washington, D.C.

Almost two centuries passed before our nation's birth certificate was given its permanent home in 1952. The Declaration of Independence, signed by 56 members of the Second Continental Congress in 1776, was to travel thousands of miles by almost every conceivable mode of transportation. Considering its nomadic existence and the abuse and neglect it suffered over many years, it is practically a miracle that it survives today.

The Declaration of Independence was adopted in Philadelphia July 4, 1776, and printed copies were distributed immediately throughout the thirteen colonies. These copies bore only the names of John Hancock, President of the Congress, and Charles Thomson, its secretary. It was not until a month later that a copy, inscribed by hand on sheepskin, was presented to the Congress for signing. This unique document was then placed in the custody of Charles Thomson.

Before the end of 1776 the travels of the Declaration of Independence had begun. With British forces closing in on Philadelphia, Congress moved to Baltimore, taking along all its important records, including the Declaration, in a baggage wagon. The following spring Congress returned to Philadelphia, but in the autumn of 1777 again fled as the Redcoats occupied the city. This time Congress met briefly in Lancaster, Pennsylvania, then moved farther west to York. York served as the nation's temporary capital for eight months until the British withdrew from Philadelphia, enabling Congress and the document to return to Independence Hall.

Following a rest of nearly five years in the venerable building where it had been adopted and signed, the famed roll of parchment once again was forced to take to the road. In June of 1783 it was not the British who were threatening Congress, but disgruntled American soldiers marching on Independence Hall with complaints chiefly against Pennsylvania's government. To avoid trouble, Congress packed up and moved to Nassau Hall in Princeton, New Jersey, for a four-month stay. Later it met in both Annapolis and Trenton, then, in 1785, took up residence in New York.

In 1789, with the inauguration of George Washington and the formation of a new government under the Constitution, the Continental Congress ceased to exist. Its records were turned over to the new administration, the Declaration of Independence going to the Secretary of State. As Thomas Jefferson was the first to hold that office, for three years the famous document was in the possession of its author. He took it back to Philadelphia when the government returned there in 1790 for a ten-year stay while Washington, D.C., then called Federal City, was rising beside the Potomac River.

When the seat of government moved to Washington in 1800 the Declaration went along by ship. In Washington it had several homes until the British again threatened the security of the document toward the end of the War of 1812 and it went into hiding in nearby Virginia. Secretary of State James Monroe ordered his department's records loaded onto carts and rushed across the Potomac. While the torch was being put to Washington's public buildings, the Declaration was safely stored in a private home in Leesburg, Virginia.

Back again in Washington, after the British fleet had sailed out of Chesapeake Bay, the roll of parchment moved wherever the State Department moved, until 1841, when it went on display in the new Patent Office Building at the request of Secretary of State Daniel Webster. For 35 years it hung on a wall there, unprotected from the sun and from changes in temperature. For the nation's 100th birthday celebration in 1876 President Grant permitted it to be taken to Philadelphia by train and exhibited to thousands of admiring Americans, many of whom expressed alarm at its poor condition. On its return the Declaration was displayed in the new State, War and Navy Building next door to the White House, a fortuitous decision, as its old home in the Patent Office Building was destroyed by fire shortly after the move. By 1894 the 118-year-old document had deteriorated so badly that a decision was made to lock it in a safe away from all light.

This seclusion continued for more than a quarter of a century. Then it was decided that with proper care and lighting America's most famous roll of parchment again could be safely shown to the public. In 1924 it went on display in the Library of Congress, brought there in a mail truck. Its stay on Capitol Hill was interrupted when the attack on Pearl Harbor on December 7, 1941, made the safety of any building in Washington dubious. A trip via Pullman car transported it to the protection of an underground vault at Fort Knox, Kentucky, for a three-year stay.

After several more years on display at the Library of Congress, the Declaration of Independence began its last journey, a short one. On December 13, 1952, with great ceremony, it was removed from the Library of Congress and placed in an army tank which transported it to the bronze and marble shrine prepared for it at the new National Archives Building about a mile away.

11

"I, BENJAMIN FRANKLIN . . ."

The death of Benjamin Franklin on April 17, 1790, and the probating a week later of his will and the unusual codicil attached to it, set in motion a unique long-range philanthropy. The lengthy document beginning "I, Benjamin Franklin, of Philadelphia, printer, late Minister Plenipotentiary from the United States of America to the Court of France, now President of the State of Pennsylvania, do make and declare . . ." has benefitted thousands of Franklin's fellow Americans for nearly two centuries and has yet to run its course.

Although closely associated with Philadelphia during his entire adult life, Benjamin Franklin was born in Boston, in 1706. He learned the printer's trade there before leaving home at the age of seventeen to find employment in Philadelphia. In the codicil to his will he directed that these two cities share alike in an exceptional form of generosity that was to go into effect within one year after his demise:

I have considered that among Artisans good Apprentices are most likely to make good Citizens, and having myself been bred to a manual Art Printing, in my native Town, and afterwards assisted to set up my business in Philadelphia by kind loan of Money from two Friends there, which was the foundation of my Fortune, and of all the utility in life that may be ascribed to me, I wish to be useful even after my Death, if possible, in forming and advancing other young men that may be serviceable to their Country in both those Towns.

To this End I devote Two thousand Pounds Sterling, which I give, one thousand thereof to the Inhabitants of the Town of Boston, in Massachusetts, and the other thousand to the Inhabitants of the City of Philadelphia, in Trust and for the Uses, Interests and Purposes hereinafter mentioned and declared.

Franklin then stipulated that in each place the money was to be loaned at five percent interest per year to young married artificers under 25 years of age who wished to set themselves up in business. Loans to any one person were not to exceed 60 pounds nor be less than 15 pounds. In addition to paying interest, the borrower would be obligated to return one-tenth of the principal each year so that money could be loaned to new applicants.

Looking far down the road, Franklin estimated, in fact seemed to expect, that within one hundred years the two funds would have grown to 131,000 pounds each. He asked that in each case the 31,000 pounds be continued as a loan fund for another one hundred years. As for the two remaining sums of 100,000 pounds, they were to go to the respective cities and be used for the public good. He had his own ideas about the kind of improvements Boston and Philadelphia might make with the money, even one hundred years later. He suggested that in Boston it go for "Public Works which may be judged of most general utility to the Inhabitants such as Fortifications, Bridges, Aqueducts, Public Buildings, Baths, Pavements or whatever may make Living in the Town more convenient to its People and render it more agreeable to strangers, resorting thither for Health or a temporary residence."

Franklin's suggestions for Philadelphia were more

specific. He pointed out that the continued construction of buildings and pavements would eventually cause rainwater to run off rather than soak into the ground, thus causing wells to dry up. Therefore, he recommended that if it had not been done sooner, at the end of one hundred years some of the 100,000 pounds be used for building a dam on Wissahickon Creek and piping water into the city. The remainder of the money, he suggested, could be used to improve navigation on the Schuylkill River, which flows into the Delaware in south Philadelphia.

Having planned the disposition of his legacy for the first hundred years, Franklin addressed himself very briefly to what should be done at the end of the second hundred, which incidentally, will be in 1991. He estimated that by then the 31,000 pounds in each of the two revolving loan funds would have grown to 4,061,000 pounds. He directed that in each case one quarter go to the city and three quarters to the state, each to use its share as it pleased.

It may be of interest to review briefly how Franklin's plan worked out.

As one might imagine, over a period of almost two hundred years, things have not gone exactly as Franklin would have liked. Long before the first hundred years had ended, the industrial system of the country had changed so radically that apprentices in the various trades no longer applied for loans. At times, too, the going interest rate fell below that set by Franklin. Fortunately, those charged with administering his gift were able from time to time to go to court and obtain changes in the rules and thus continue distributing his largess to deserving residents of the two municipalities which he favored.

In Philadelphia, the Benjamin Franklin Fund is administered by a body known as the Board of Directors of City Trusts. When the board took over, in 1869, the Franklin Fund totaled only about $40,000 instead of a sum six times as large which Franklin had counted on. He had not allowed for long periods when the money lay completely idle nor for numerous loans that never were repaid.

The new management felt that the restriction requiring borrowers to be under 25 years of age was a serious disadvantage. Through a court order they raised it to 35, which increased the number of loan applicants, but only for a short time. However, in 1890, when the fund totaled about $100,000, the board agreed to carry out Franklin's wishes and set aside $76,000 for public works and leave $24,000 in the loan fund. The first-named amount was kept until 1908, then with accrued interest, which brought it up to $133,000, it was presented to the Franklin Institute Building Fund, which eventually erected a fitting monument to the great man—the Institute's complex in central Philadelphia housing an outstanding museum of science and a planetarium.

In spite of periods of active solicitation by the board, the loan fund remained completely inactive from 1885 to 1939. The old apprenticeship system had disappeared, and young mechanics found no advantage in borrowing under the terms offered. From time to time the administrators obtained court orders liberalizing the loan terms. Today the fund makes 30-year first mortgage loans on Philadelphia real estate for as much as $10,000 at interest rates one-half percent below the maximum allowed by law. The value of the fund, at the close of 1975, was $685,000.

The managers of Boston's Franklin Fund (now incorporated as The Franklin Foundation) encountered much the same problems. Social and industrial changes seemed to negate the rules laid down by the founder. After 1836 the lending rate fell to less than one loan a year and none at all was made from 1886 until 1962. However, as early as 1819 the managers, mindful of the founder's hope "that no part of the Money will at any time lie dead," began investing most of the fund with the Massachusetts Hospital Life Insurance Company, which ran a prototype of the modern mutual fund. Thus, in January of 1894 the managers were able to turn over to the city the rather handsome sum of $329,300 for the public works and retain $102,085 in the loan fund. Eleven years passed before a decision was made on how best to use the larger amount. Meanwhile, interest had increased it to $408,000.

At this point Henry J. Pritchett, manager of the fund, visited Andrew Carnegie and received a promise of matching funds for an educational institution similar to New York's Cooper Union, provided the City of Boston would contribute the land. A site was donated at the corner of Berkeley and Appleton streets in downtown Boston, and on September 21, 1908, the Franklin Union opened its doors. Initially it offered only evening courses in science and engineering for young men and women employed in the daytime. A few years later day courses were added. In 1941 the name was changed to Franklin Technical Institute and in 1961 to Franklin Institute of Boston. Today it is a two-year technical college, with programs leading to the degree of Associate in Engineering as well as other technical programs. It is supported by admission fees, endowments and gifts.

In 1962 The Franklin Foundation secured a court decree authorizing loans on easy terms for medical training, thereby reviving, after a lapse of over a century, Franklin's intention that his accumulating fund should "form and advance young men that may be serviceable to their country"; such loans being currently made to third- and fourth-year students attending medical schools in the Boston area—Boston University, Harvard and Tufts. This loan program was made possible by the generosity of a Boston doctor, Dr. Louis E. Wolfson, who set up a separate fund of $100,000 to guarantee the Franklin Fund against losses on such loans. By June 30, 1975, over 1,700 young men and women had been thus aided, and the Franklin Fund had reached $2,811,000, of which $1,998,000 was in medical training loans.

From the way things are going it would appear that in 1991 Boston and the Commonwealth of Massachusetts may be dividing close to five million dollars to build additional useful monuments to an outstanding American who had a profound concern for his fellow man.

BATTLE OF THE PIGTAIL

Mid-1970's news accounts of American soldiers in West Germany facing court-martial rather than have their hair cut might be said to be a replay of earlier United States history. Back in 1801 the military published a hair length edict. However, at that time it was not only enlisted men who objected to visiting the barber. A veteran infantry officer of Irish descent, Colonel Thomas Butler, Jr., staged a bizarre one-man mutiny over the matter.

Colonel Butler was a Revolutionary War hero who had participated in virtually every major battle fought in the middle states. For meritorious conduct at Brandywine he had been thanked on the battlefield by General George Washington. At the close of the war he married and took up farming at Carlisle, Pennsylvania. Reentering the service in 1791, Butler saw action in Colonel Arthur St. Clair's disastrous Indian campaign in Ohio and the Whiskey Rebellion in western Pennsylvania. In 1797 President Washington sent him to Tennessee, where he successfully resolved a dispute over Indian lands being unlawfully entered by white settlers.

In 1801 fate made Colonel Butler the leading character in a curious drama. Thomas Jefferson had just been elected President. It was no secret that the new President disliked all badges of aristocracy, all customs and practices that smacked of a monarchial past. One of these practices evidenced in the armed forces was the wearing of a queue— a braid of long hair worn hanging in the back, usually tied with a ribbon. Therefore it is not too surprising that the commanding general of the army, James Wilkinson, possibly on orders from the new President, at least with his obvious approval, directed that the beribboned pigtails of the military be cut off, ostensibly for sanitary reasons.

Wilkinson's order abolished a custom in military hair styling that was more than a century old. Even though men of all ranks voiced strenuous objections, there was nothing they could do about it. Even though they complained bitterly that having their locks shorn made them look like convicts, with one notable exception they bowed to the inevitable.

The exception was Colonel Thomas Butler, who refused outright to conform. Highly regarded by his fellow officers, including General Wilkinson, and only fifty-three years of age, which meant he could still have a long career ahead of him, he nevertheless was determined to have his own way in this touchy matter. Wilkinson's reaction was to grant him an indulgence and overlook the matter.

Two years went by. Wilkinson paid a visit to Fort Adams, at Natchez, Mississippi, where Butler was stationed. For reasons not too clear today, a bitter controversy developed between the two officers. This resulted in the General withdrawing his indulgence and ordering Colonel Butler placed under arrest and court-martialed, not only for not obeying the order relating to haircuts but on various other charges. Butler appealed directly to the President who refused to intervene, and also enlisted the support of an influential old friend, Andrew Jackson, which also availed nothing. The trial took place in November of 1803. Butler was found guilty of disobeying the regulation about hair styles but defended himself successfully on other counts.

Following the trial, Butler remained under arrest for nearly six months. Wilkinson finally ordered him released and assigned to duty in New Orleans, with the stipulation that he "leave his tail behind him."

Butler ignored this condition. Instead of applying the shears he began a vigorous campaign to find out why he was being harassed. He again appealed to Andrew Jackson, who approached the President and Congress with a petition signed by prominent citizens of Nashville. By now, Wilkinson's dander was up, too. He brought the recalcitrant colonel before another court-martial in July 1805. This time Colonel Butler was found guilty of disobeying orders and mutinous conduct. Suspension of pay and relief from command for one year was the recommendation made by the court to Wilkinson.

Things looked bad for Revolutionary War hero Butler. Even so, he had the last word. Before the papers reached Wilkinson, Butler died of yellow fever. Aware that the end was in sight, he had planned a coup with his friends, one final gesture of defiance. He told them: "Bore a hole through the bottom of my coffin, right under my head, and let my queue hang down through it, that the d____d old rascal may see that, even when dead, I refuse to obey his orders."

Washington Crossing the Delaware, painted by Emanuel Leutze in 1851, is a famous representation of a great moment in the struggle for American Independence. But the painting's accuracy has been questioned by many critics.

Some have said that it is far-fetched that Washington would have been standing in a rowboat on a storm-tossed river in a sleet storm. But, having the main figure standing was the style the artists of the era used. Also, the flag shown was not used until 1777, a year later.

It is interesting to note that Leutze, who grew up in Philadelphia, painted the scene in his Dusseldorf, Germany, studio with the Rhine as his backdrop and art students as models.

Someone once said that the first man to eat an oyster must have had plenty of courage. But how about the first man to load a sailing vessel with blocks of crystal-clear ice, cut from a pond not far from Lynn, Massachusetts, and to send it off to a remote, sun-drenched island in the West Indies?

This seemingly foolish venture was initiated by Frederic Tudor, a young Bostonian, in February 1806. For even attempting such an outlandish project, his friends considered him daft. Luckily this view was not shared by the bankers who lent him the $10,000 to buy the brig *Favorite*. His crew did, however, share in the belief that Tudor must be crazed. They wondered how the vessel would be able to transport the ice more than 2,000 miles to St. Pierre on the island of Martinique without their unique cargo melting and filling the hold with water.

But Tudor was right. Most of his ice arrived in the tropics intact. Although he lost money on this first shipment, the young entrepreneur met and overcame a number of both financial and physical obstacles upon returning to Boston. He remained hard at work solving the various problems connected with the shipping of ice and the storing of ice in warm climates with a minimal amount of loss due to melting.

Following the end of the War of 1812 and its shipping embargo, Tudor developed a profitable trade with several Caribbean islands. He also began supplying Charleston, South Carolina, and New Orleans, Louisiana, with his most unusual commodity.

In 1833, to the astonishment of much of the maritime world, a vessel of Tudor's loaded with ice put into the harbor at Calcutta, then the capital of British India.

Tudor's success brought on the inevitable competitors and with them came expansion and innovations in the ice-shipping business. During 1856, according to the Boston

Board of Trade, 146,000 tons of ice were shipped from the Hub to fifty-three ports around the world, some as far away from Boston as those in China and Australia.

Although ice eventually paid off handsomely for Tudor, he lost a great deal of money in other speculations. One such futile attempt at money-making was an experiment he made dealing with the preservation of fruit by refrigeration. Not until he was sixty-five was he out of debt and able to enjoy the riches that his efforts had brought him. In 1864, Tudor died at the age of eighty, one of Boston's and America's mercantile heroes.

The business of shipping natural ice long distances, which owed its very existence to Tudor's aggressiveness and bulldog tenacity, flourished for a little longer than a decade after the Civil War. Then a gradual decline in demand for natural ice became evident as methods for producing cheap, artificially made ice were developed in various parts of the world. By the early 1900's, the harvesting of natural ice from lakes and ponds on a large scale was becoming a thing of the past.

One successful holdout against the artificial ice machine was another New England enterprise called the Maine Lake Ice Company of Sargentville, Maine. This company carried on a thriving natural ice trade from 1900 until 1916 shipping blocks of ice weighing, on the average, 430 pounds each. The ice was cut in the winter from the frozen surface of Walker's Pond, stored in huge icehouses on the pond's edge and then sent chiefly to the Baltimore-Washington, D.C. area in sturdy four- and five-masted sailing vessels.

Insofar as consumption of ice in the home was concerned, artificially made ice enjoyed only a brief career. Within the first twenty-five years of the 20th century, mechanical home refrigeration was taking over. The ice wagon and the iceman's wrought iron tongs, being virtually eliminated by progress, went to the museum, vanquished by that marvelous machine, the refrigerator.

ROYALTY IN EXILE

A rather small town in the United States once numbered an ex-king among its residents for nearly two decades. The distinguished resident of Bordentown, New Jersey, was Joseph Bonaparte, brother of the great Napoleon, and his senior by one year. Before settling down in America to the quiet life of a country gentleman, Joseph had occupied two European thrones. In 1806 Emperor Napoleon I, in keeping with his custom of bestowing crowns on close relatives, had proclaimed his brother Joseph king of Naples. Two years later Joseph was promoted to the thankless job of king of Spain, where his five-year reign was a stormy one. Twice he had to leave Madrid before the onslaught of hostile armies. In 1813 he fled from Spain for good and the next year retired. After Napoleon's defeat in 1815, Joseph departed for refuge in the United States, arriving at New York harbor in August 1815.

The famous visitor came without his wife Julie, who preferred to stay in Europe. His two daughters also remained behind, although both later came to stay with their father on extended visits.

While in power Joseph had been able to acquire many properties in Europe as well as art treasures and precious jewels. Thus he was able to buy a 211-acre estate called Point Breeze near Bordentown (which eventually grew to 1,700 acres) with a network of bridle paths, underground tunnels between buildings, many statues and a man-made lake. The house in which he entertained distinguished travelers, among them Marquis de Lafayette, was a museum in itself; priceless furniture, carpets and tapestries graced the many rooms, and the paintings on display included masterpieces by Rubens, Titian, Murillo, Velazquez, Raphael and David.

Joseph Bonaparte's American mistress, Annette Savage, was a fiery brunette whose origin (Quaker gentlewoman or Indian maiden?) has been the subject of much conjecture. She and Joseph had two daughters, one of whom died in infancy. The other, Caroline, born in 1819, grew to womanhood.

When Caroline was five she and her mother went to Paris, where Annette married a silk merchant who was either chosen by her or provided by Joseph. Alexis de la Folie accompanied Annette and Caroline to America and eventually he and Annette had five children.

In 1820 a heartbreaking fire destroyed the Point Breeze house, but Bonaparte's servants and neighbors braved the flames to save most of the paintings and furniture. He appears to have been amazed that there was no looting. This courage, honesty and friendship impressed Joseph deeply, and he wrote a note of thanks to the people of Bordentown full of his admiration for them and his faith in the basic goodness of man.

This was not an impassioned outburst brought about just by the fire, for Joseph Bonaparte was known for his generosity and his kind nature. It was said that in him flowered many of the human virtues which seemed lacking in his more illustrious brother, and he was well-liked by the Americans he had come to know. After the fire a new mansion was constructed on the Point Breeze estate and a second building was erected for visitors.

After seventeen years in America, Joseph learned that although as a Bonaparte he was still barred from France, he was free to live in England. He was now 64 and homesick for Europe. In 1832 he sailed for England, with his many American friends bidding a sad adieu to their royal neighbor.

Revelry was part of Mackinac Island's spring in 1822. Thousands of Indians and French-Canadian voyageurs had returned from their winter quest for furs. After the clerks of the American Fur Company appraised the pelts and grudgingly parted with money equal to one third of their worth, the fun began. The trappers' newly found wealth immediately changed hands as they emptied their pockets at the nearby company store. The Indians purchased trinkets and whiskey, the French-Canadians bought high hats and whiskey. The result was a company store which resounded with convivial boasts of the snaring of rare pelts, the adventures met along the route and the heavy loads carried over portages.

One of the men, while recounting his experiences, became so exuberant that the gun in his hand went off. The full blast of duck shot and powder lodged in the stomach of nineteen-year-old Alexis St. Martin. The young voyageur fell to the floor and a cry went up for a doctor. Fortunately, one arrived quickly, pushed back the vital organs protruding through the gaping wound, picked out bits of shattered ribs, bound up the youth's abdomen and started him on the road to a miraculous recovery.

The doctor was William Beaumont, a U.S. Army surgeon stationed at Fort Mackinac on Mackinac Island, where Lake Huron meets Lake Michigan. Born in 1785 in Lebanon, Connecticut, he had no formal medical training but served a medical apprenticeship with a St. Albans, Vermont, doctor and began his career on the battlefields of the War of 1812 along the U.S.-Canada border.

Beaumont was not only a capable surgeon but one with an inquiring mind. As St. Martin's external wounds healed, Beaumont observed that the stomach became attached to the chest wall and a small aperture, about the size of a penny, opened directly into the stomach. Beaumont realized that here was a rare opportunity to study the digestive processes of the human body, a mystery to science at that time. When the community ran out of funds to support the convalescing voyageur, the doctor and his bride of a year took the youth into their home and, as Alexis slowly regained his health, Beaumont began conducting experiments through this "window."

Nature cooperated by providing a small interior flap that kept the contents of Alexis' stomach from spilling out under normal conditions but which could easily be pushed aside with a finger for experimental purposes. Dr. Beaumont inserted samples of various foodstuffs attached to silk thread, retrieving them for study at planned intervals. He extracted samples of gastric juice and, keeping them at body temperature in glass containers, studied the reaction upon particles of food. He could insert thermometers and even look through the opening directly into the stomach cavity.

In 1825, after exhaustive experiments, Beaumont published his findings in a medical journal, disproving commonly held beliefs that the stomach was either a grinding mill or a fermenting vat. His experiments, he said, "demonstrate that the stomach secretes a fluid which possesses solvent properties. The change in solid substances is effected too rapidly to be accounted for on the principle of either maceration or putrefaction."

The strange relationship between doctor and patient was not always a happy one. As Alexis regained his strength, he began to object to the experiments. Beaumont, in his zeal to collect information, rarely considered Alexis' feelings and was generally undiplomatic and often short-tempered. His patient constantly longed to return to his former trade and only grudgingly submitted to the wearisome experimenting. But they worked together for several years before Alexis, hungry for the freedom he had known, disappeared. He returned to his home in Montreal, married, and went to work for the Hudson's Bay Company. Several years passed before Beaumont had word of him. With the help of company officials, he was persuaded to return, bringing his wife and two children for Beaumont to support.

After a vacation trip to Montreal in 1831, Alexis once

more joined Dr. Beaumont, now stationed at Plattsburgh, New York, for another round of experiments. This time they even traveled together to Washington and Boston, where Alexis was exhibited before some of the best medical minds of the nation. In response to invitations from scientific societies in France, Beaumont planned to take his partner there. But it was not to be. In 1834 Alexis decided he had had enough and said goodbye forever to the bothersome business of having his insides explored in the interests of medical science. He paddled his canoe back to Canada and refused to cooperate with science again. He lived to be eighty-six, carrying with him to his grave one more bodily orifice than Mother Nature had given him.

Meanwhile Beaumont gained international fame by publishing the results of 238 experiments in a volume titled *Experiments and Observations on the Gastric Juice and the Physiology of Digestion.* His discoveries opened a new era in the study of the stomach and its functions. His unwavering pursuit of facts prompted the distinguished physician Sir William Osler to call him the first great American physiologist.

In 1874 a young Texas doctor named John Burke treated a patient suffering from typhoid fever. The patient recovered and, upon leaving, promised the doctor that he would someday repay him.

After a few years the doctor moved to another town. One day when walking to his office, he noticed a group of horsemen heading towards the bank. He realized that they were robbers and that the leader was his former patient.

After a few minutes of pleading by the doctor that he and the entire town would suffer if the men carried out their plan, the band of men rode out of town on their leader's orders. With this, the patient had repaid his long-overdue debt.

The bandit leader was none other than Frank James, brother of the notorious outlaw Jesse James.

A CLOSE CALL
FOR LAFAYETTE

No foreign dignitary visiting America ever received, before or since, as warm a welcome as that given the Marquis de Lafayette when he came back in mid-August of 1824 for a last look at the country for which he fought, for which he even bled when a British ball struck him at the Battle of Brandywine. The celebration for the gallant Frenchman, who had suffered with the Continental troops at Valley Forge and contributed greatly to the American victory at Yorktown, extended almost without letup for a solid year.

A Lafayette biographer, Andreas Latzko, summed up in *Lafayette: A Life,* the high regard citizens of the growing new nation had for the man who had been almost as close as a son to General George Washington:

Everybody knew, and could appreciate from his own experience, the privations Lafayette had endured at Valley Forge, snowbound in his canvas tent in the virgin forest. This rich French count had voluntarily abandoned the paradise of Versailles to endure these privations in winter quarters and had shed his young blood at Brandywine for the liberation of the American people; and he was idolized for it. There still lived up and down the country a few veterans of the War of Independence, but none of them had been a general at twenty and an intimate friend of George Washington! To the people of the United States Lafayette was not merely a guest: he seemed like a witness arisen from the grave to tell of the glorious past, almost a saint. The farmers came in from many miles around the still widely separated towns; women asked a saintly blessing on their children; there burst from twenty million hearts a tornado of gratitude which knew no cessation until Lafayette departed again from America.

He spent his sixty-seventh and sixty-eighth birthdays as the guest of the New World, and every morning, noonday and evening between these two signposts of his life was a link in a single unbroken chain of public receptions, welcomes and farewells, banquets, toasts, celebrations! Escorted from town to town, intercepted by waiting crowds at every posting house, the sixty-seven-year-old veteran of the fight for freedom covered almost the whole continent from north to south and east to west. Only occasionally was he able to take three or four days' rest, on the country estates of his best friends, and even during these rare breaks he had to shake hands and exchange friendly words with hundreds of admirers who flocked in from all around. Every house that gave him a night's shelter became a place of pilgrimage, and he could not refuse the homage of the good people who brought their children with them on horseback from hundreds of miles away, so that their far descendants should be able to say with pride that their forefathers had seen the great Lafayette face to face.

At the time of Lafayette's arrival, all travel had to be by carriage or by boat. Contrary to biographer Latzko's flattering tribute to the Frenchman's stamina, General Lafayette did not cover "almost the whole continent." Nevertheless, in addition to visiting old battlefields and old friends, he made a point of going to every one of the states that then made up the Union, twenty-four in all, including two—Louisiana and Missouri—that lay west of the Mississippi River.

He visited with two Presidents—James Monroe, an old comrade-in-arms of Revolutionary War days who had invited him to the United States as the guest of the government, and John Quincy Adams, who was sworn into office during Lafayette's stay in America. Three former Presidents also were on his visiting list—John Adams, Thomas Jefferson and James Madison. He also found time for a call on an old friend from home, Joseph Bonaparte, brother of the great Napoleon, once king of Naples and king of Spain and now living in exile on his luxurious estate near Bordentown, New Jersey.[1]

A high spot of the year-long visit was the generous action Congress took in December of 1824. The hero from abroad was voted a Christmas present of $200,000 in cash and 24,000 acres of public land. The low spot came when the general and his party, which consisted of his only son, middle-aged George Washington Lafayette, secretary Levasseur and valet Bastien, met with an accident that could easily have had tragic results for all four.

A tour through the South had brought the travelers to New Orleans in the spring of 1825. Following the usual round of dinners and ceremonies there, they boarded a Mississippi River steamboat for a trip upstream to St. Louis. From this bustling frontier outpost they came back down the Mississippi to the mouth of the Ohio River and turned eastward, bound for Louisville and Cincinnati. A side trip up the Cumberland River took them to Nashville to spend a few days with another military hero, Andrew Jackson, who in another four years would become the seventh President of the United States. At Nashville, Governor William Carroll of Tennessee joined the voyagers for the rest of the trip to Louisville.

Mississippi River steamboats—flat-bottomed, snub-nosed and with all their machinery on the lower deck—were the latest American invention. In service for less than

[1]For the story of Joseph Bonaparte's exile in New Jersey, read *Royalty In Exile* on page 22.

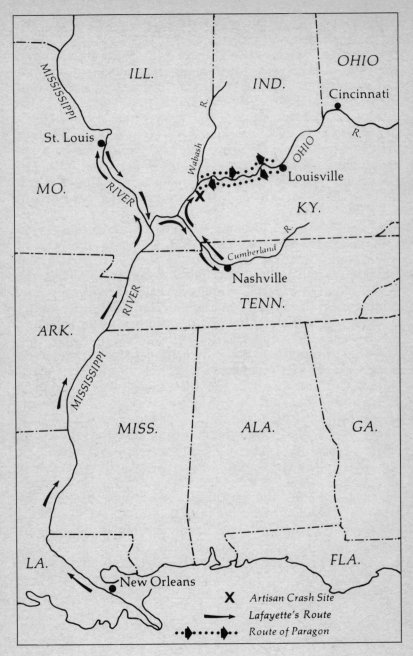

MISSISSIPPI

ILL.

IND.

OHIO

Cincinnati

St. Louis

R.

Wabash

OHIO

R.

Louisville

MO.

RIVER

KY.

X

R.

Cumberland

Nashville

RIVER

TENN.

ARK.

MISSISSIPPI

MISS.

ALA.

GA.

LA.

FLA.

New Orleans

X   *Artisan Crash Site*

    Lafayette's Route

    Route of Paragon

ten years, they were something entirely new for the French visitors. The party found the river trip a pleasant change from carriage travel. Lafayette also found it afforded him time to begin answering an ever-growing pile of letters from well-wishers.

Although neither the Mississippi nor the Ohio had navigation lights in those early days of steamboating, the captains in charge of the general's journey seemed to have no misgivings about pushing ahead on the darkest of nights. May 8, 1825, was such a night, and the crowded steamboat *Artisan* chugged along smoothly on the calm waters of the Ohio, carrying Lafayette and an assemblage of his admirers upstream toward Louisville. The general, his son and his secretary occupied the "Ladies Cabin" in the stern of the boat, a dozen steps down from the main deck.

Virtually everyone but the crew had retired after a leisurely afternoon of watching the forested hills of Illinois and Kentucky glide by. About midnight, as the *Artisan* drew close to the mouth of the Wabash, a shock suddenly went through her, upsetting furniture and tumbling sleepers from their berths. Lafayette's secretary, Auguste Levasseur, ran up on deck and learned from the captain that they had struck a "snag," an underwater obstruction of some sort. Water was pouring into the forward hold. He hurried back to the cabin to find the general being dressed by his valet Bastien. In Levasseur's journal, *Lafayette in America,* published in 1829, he described the scene:

'What news?' said he (Lafayette), on seeing me enter. 'That we shall go to the bottom, general, if we cannot extricate ourselves, and we have not a moment to spare.' And I immediately began to collect my papers, which I threw pell-mell into my port-folio; George Lafayette on his part, hastily collected those objects he thought most necessary to his father, and begged him to follow us, but his toilet not being yet made, he wished us to go first and provide means of escape. 'What!' cried his son, 'do you think that in such circumstances we will leave you for a moment?' and immediately we each seized a hand and dragged him towards the door. He followed us, smiling at our haste, and began to ascend with us, but had scarcely reached the middle of the stairs, when he perceived he had forgotten his snuff-box, ornamented with a picture of Washington, and wished to return for it; I went to the end of the cabin, found it and brought it to him.

At this time the rolling of the vessel was so violent and irregular, and the tumult over our heads augmented to such a degree, that I believed we should not have time to escape before she sunk. At last, we reached the deck, where all the passengers were in the greatest confusion, some bringing their trunks, others looking for the boat, and crying out for Lafayette. He was already in the midst of them, but owing to the darkness of the night, no one recognised him; the boat heeled so much to starboard that it was with difficulty we could keep our footing on the deck.

The captain assisted by two sailors, had brought his boat to this side, and I heard his sonorous voice crying out, Lafayette! Lafayette! but we could not reach him on account of the confusion around us. Nevertheless the vessel heeled more and more, each moment augmented the danger, we felt that it was time to make a last effort, and pushed into the middle of the crowd, where I cried, 'here is General Lafayette!' This exclamation produced the effect I anticipated. The most profound silence succeeded to the confusion, a free passage was opened for us, and all those who were ready to spring into the boat, spontaneously checked themselves, not wishing to think of their own safety before that of Lafayette was ascertained.

Over the general's protestations, they got him into the boat and he and Levasseur were rowed the short distance to the heavily-forested riverbank. When he realized his son was not with him, he became violently agitated. The secretary's journal continues.

He began to call, George! George! with all his strength, but his voice was drowned by the cries which arose from the vessel, and by the terrible noise made by the steam escaping from the engine, and received no answer. In vain, to re-assure him, I represented to him that his son was a good swimmer, and that he doubtless had remained on board voluntarily, and with his coolness he would escape all danger. Nothing had any effect; he continued to traverse the shore calling on George.

Forty-five-year-old George Washington Lafayette was safe enough and cooly aiding the other passengers. In due time he and valet Bastien came ashore with the rest. Some saved themselves by swimming. Fortunately, no one was drowned. They gathered on the bank to warm themselves around several fires.

Meanwhile the *Artisan* had settled to the bottom but in fairly shallow water. When daylight came, the small boat began plying back and forth to bring off whatever could be salvaged. While most of the general's baggage was recovered, out of about two hundred letters ready for the post, all but about sixty were lost. Governor Carroll of Tennessee, in true frontier fashion, pitched in to help with the salvage operation, much to the amazement of urbane secretary Levasseur.

At daybreak they recommenced their trips to the vessel to save some of the baggage and to procure food. The captain, the governor of Tennessee, and a young Virginian, Mr. Crawford, directed these searches with great activity. It was a singular and touching event to see the governor of a state, that is to say, the first magistrate of a republic, without shoes, stockings, or a hat, doing the duty of a boatman as if it had been his real occupation, and that much more for the benefit of others than for himself, for he had very little on board to lose by the shipwreck.

The search parties discovered food and drink, and the sun came out, all of which, according to Levasseur, put an entirely different face on the matter.

These different searches obtained us a trunk belonging to the general, in which were his most valuable papers, and a small part of the passengers' baggage. They also brought a leg of smoked venison, some biscuits, a case of claret, and a keg of Madeira. With these provisions, about fifty men, for such was our number, repaired their strength, exhausted by a night of labor and anxiety.

The day, on its return, shone on an interesting picture. The shore was covered with wrecks (debris) of all kinds, in the midst of which each eagerly searched for their own property; some mournfully recounted the extent of their losses, others could not avoid laughing at the nakedness or costume in which they found themselves; this gaiety soon became prevalent, and pleasantries circulated around the fires of our bivouac, and at last smoothed the visages of the most sorrowful, and almost transformed our shipwreck into a party of pleasure.

The rescue of these travelers shipwrecked in the wilderness reads almost like a fairy tale. Not long after the sun came up, another steamboat, the *Paragon* out of Louisville, appeared on the scene, heading for New Orleans with a cargo of whiskey and tobacco. By a very lucky coincidence one of the members of the shipwrecked group was part owner of the *Paragon*. He had the boat turned around, and soon the castaways again were on their way to Louisville. After a few days rest there, Lafayette and his companions continued on to Cincinnati.

At the end of May the indefatigable hero was viewing the wonders of Niagara Falls. And after more traveling, interrupted by frequent ceremonies and celebrations, he reached Boston on June 15, just in time to catch his breath before laying the cornerstone of the Bunker Hill Monument two days later.

Lafayette's American tour was scheduled to end August 13, just two days short of a full year. The General planned to return home on a passenger ship, but as the time drew near word came that Uncle Sam would be pleased to send him home on a brand new frigate, the *Brandywine,* if he could delay his departure for a few weeks until the vessel was ready for sea. The General gladly did so. The day after a combination farewell/birthday dinner at the White House, Lafayette boarded the *Brandywine* bound for Le Havre.

34

Over two hundred years ago Wolfgang von Kempelen, an engineering expert attached to the court of Vienna, demonstrated an elaborate toy he had created to a select audience which included Empress Maria Theresa of Hungary. This toy, an automaton chess player known as the Turk, thus began a public career of entertaining and mystifying chess enthusiasts which lasted almost 75 years.

At the insistence of the Hungarian royal family, Kempelen began exhibiting the unusual Turk who won most of its matches against the best players of Europe. On Kempelen's death in 1804 the automaton was acquired by Johann Maelzel, another mechanical wizard. Noted for his showmanship, Maelzel successfully exhibited his wonderful machine in Europe's large cities. In 1826 he brought the Turk to America, where for more than a decade it attracted throngs of people.

The Turk was a wooden mannequin resembling a character from *The Thousand and One Nights,* as he was dressed in a colorful robe and a thickly wrapped, plumed turban. He sat cross-legged on a backless chair.

Before him was a wooden cabinet containing a complex mass of mechanical parts. An inlaid chess board formed the top of the cabinet. The Turk's only movable part was his left arm. When Maelzel pulled the switch, the Turk would move his left arm amid the clang of moving mechanical gears and his fingers would pick up and deposit the chess pieces. Before each exhibition, Maelzel would open all of the doors of the cabinet to convince the audience that the cabinet contained only machinery. The Turk's live opponent had his own chess board on another table. Maelzel moved back and forth between the two boards, repeating the Turk's moves on the opponent's board and vice versa.

Edgar Allan Poe witnessed several of the Turk's performances at Richmond, Va., and, like everyone else who saw a demonstration, attempted to unravel the intricacies of the amazing machine. So intrigued was Poe with his own detective work that he wrote an article, "Maelzel's Chess-Player," for the April 1836 issue of the magazine *Southern Literary Messenger*.

Poe reasoned, correctly, that the Turk was controlled by a human hidden inside the cabinet, in this case an expert chess player from France named Schlumberger whom Maelzel had brought to America. Poe commented:

There is a man, *Schlumberger,* who attends him (Maelzel) wherever he goes, but who has no ostensible occupation other than that of assisting in the packing and unpacking of the automaton. This man is about the medium size, and has a remarkable stoop in the shoulders . . . . he is never to be seen during the exhibition of the Chess-Player, although frequently visible just before and just after the exhibition. Moreover, some years ago Maelzel visited Richmond . . . *Schlumberger* was suddenly taken ill, and during his illness there was no exhibition of the Chess-Player.

Poe erroneously concluded that the hidden operator reached up inside the Turk's shoulder to manipulate the machinery that moved the pieces and at the same time watched the board through a gauze-covered window in the Turk's chest. However, the man inside actually moved the arm and fingers with an ingenious pantograph devised by Kempelen. To allow Schlumberger to follow the play, a small iron ball was suspended by a thread under each square of the board. As each chessman contained a magnet, a move to a new position would draw up the iron ball under the new square, releasing the ball under the old square. Mr. Schlumberger must have been a very busy man as well as an amazing chess player, as he rarely lost a game.

The automaton's active career came to an end in 1838 when both Maelzel and Schlumberger died of yellow fever after a trip to Havana. The taciturn Turk, veteran of thousands of chess games, eventually found a home in Philadelphia's Chinese Museum, where in 1854, at the age of 75, he perished in a fire.

HAPPINESS WAS AN OCTAGON

One of America's most bizarre architectural fads was the octagon house. Hundreds of these odd structures were built more than a century ago and, strangely enough, even though you may never have heard of an eight-sided dwelling, there probably are a hundred or so still standing today and furnishing quite adequate, if unusual, shelter for their owners.

Aside from their unconventional shape, perhaps the most curious thing about these houses was the fact that the craze for them was sparked not by an architect, but by a New York City phrenologist, Orson Squire Fowler. For those who have forgotten or those who haven't heard about it, phrenology was once an extremely popular method of character analysis and vocational guidance based on a study of the shape and protuberances of the human head.

Orson Fowler, a graduate of Amherst College in Massachusetts, was conducting a thriving business lecturing and writing books on this pseudo-science when, at the age of forty, he took up home designing as a sideline. Already an extremely popular writer, in 1848 he opened new worlds to his readers with a book setting forth very persuasively the alleged advantages of octagon-house living. He titled it *A Home for All, or a New, Cheap, Convenient, and Superior Mode of Building.* At about the same time he set an example for his followers by embarking on the construction of a huge four-story octagonal mansion at Fishkill, New York, incorporating his own advanced ideas.

Shortly thereafter, while on a lecture tour of Wisconsin, Fowler discovered another innovative builder, named Joseph Goodrich, who had constructed a house whose outside walls were formed of a mixture of water, lime, gravel and sand that hardened like rock and consequently was fireproof and ratproof. Fowler immediately applied this principle to his own Fishkill project, pouring a substance resembling concrete into wooden forms. Then in 1853, coincident with the completion of his house, he brought out a revised edition of his book with the updated title: *A Home for All, or the Gravel Wall and Octagon Mode of Building.*

The "gravel wall" portion of Fowler's crusade attracted relatively few converts. Perhaps handling a heavy, sloshy mixture on a large scale was too difficult for the average do-it-yourselfer of the 1850's. But the eight-sided house, which Fowler claimed as his own invention, was a far different story; they were built in the East, in the Midwest and even in far-off San Francisco. By the time the great man had moved into the Fishkill mansion that was to serve as headquarters for his phrenology lecturing and book publishing business, Fowler fans were busily building brick, stone and wooden octagons, using plans for various sized dwellings included in his books.

The main rooms in these far-out structures did not have peculiar shapes, as one might suppose, but usually were rectangular. Leftover triangular spaces became closets, kitchens, bathrooms and stair spaces. In the grander octagons, a circular stairway occupied the center of the house, extending from the ground floor to a glass-enclosed cupola on the roof, the latter a distinguishing feature of most octagon houses.

In addition to plugging the gravel wall and the octagon shape in his book, author Fowler expounded on virtually every phase of home building. For example, he urged separate sleeping rooms for children. His advice which follows seems as good today as when he wrote it.

Sleeping by themselves is also a first-rate plan both for health, and to prevent their imbibing anything wrong from other children; nor are their slumbers disturbed by a restless bedfellow. Nor do they keep each other awake nights, or in bed mornings, by talking. In fact, many most desirable ends does this plan subserve—at least enough to require its adoption by every parent who can afford it.

Where money was no problem, he had this suggestion for the home builder.

Most desirable, in every really good house, is a play-room for children, a gymnastic room for females, and a dancing-room.

Fowler was all for compact houses, for both functional and aesthetic reasons.

Wings on houses are not quite in as good taste as on birds. How would a little apple or peach look stuck on each side of a large one? Yet winged houses are just as disjointed and out of taste.

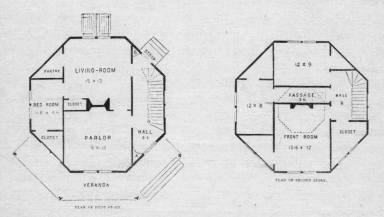

39

At the end of his book Fowler conceded that some might not care for his "gravel wall" construction. So he offered an interesting substitute which he called "board wall" construction to contrast it with the usual method of framing a house with upright members, nailing clapboard on the outside and placing laths and plastering on the inside. He suggested having boards cut five and six inches wide and from one to two inches thick. Alternately, these were laid flat with the outside edge even, one on top of the other, and each nailed to the one beneath it. A good, solid wall, to be sure. But here was the real trick. With the alternating width of the boards, one ended up with horizontal grooves for anchoring the inside plaster, thus eliminating the expense of lathing.

Fowler's own solidly-built home at Fishkill, New York, has long since disappeared. After having several owners, it eventually became a run-down eyesore known locally as "Fowler's Folly" and, in 1897, on orders from the town fathers, was destroyed by a hefty charge of dynamite.

The majority of surviving octagon houses can be seen in the northeast and north central regions of the country, predominately in New England, New York, Ohio and Michigan. However, the fad, at its peak, found its way into more than twenty states as well as Canada.

Perhaps the most striking of these unusual buildings open to the public is the brick Richards' mansion built in 1856 at Watertown, Wisconsin, thirty-five miles west of Milwaukee. Owned by the local historical society and on view from May through October, it has fifty-seven rooms (if one counts the closets and halls) and a spiral center staircase.

Just for the record, the famous red brick Octagon House in Washington, D.C., at the corner of New York Avenue and 18th Street, N.W., is not an octagon at all, but an elongated hexagon with a rounded front. Ages ago somebody unsure of his geometric forms dubbed it an octagon and the label stuck. Long headquarters of the American Institute of Architects, the building, dating from 1800, became a national historic shrine in 1970.

FRENCHMAN
UP IN THE AIR

A craze began in 1829 when Sam Patch jumped into Niagara Gorge from Goat Island, the island separating the American Falls and the Canadian, or Horseshoe, Falls and lived to tell about it.

Since then, a variety of people with a variety of contraptions have been drawn by the mystique and adventure found in the challenging and conquering of the falls.

But no daredevil who has ever braved Niagara Falls ever gained as much attention as the French tightrope walker Jean Blondin, who astounded the world in 1859 by crossing Niagara Gorge on a steel cable 1,300 feet long. Lloyd Graham in his book *Niagara Country* describes the scene:

It was late in the afternoon of June 30, 1859, when Blondin started out on his first trip across Niagara Gorge via cable. One may imagine the enormous crowds which watched nervously from every vantage point on both the Cana-

41

dian and American edges of the gorge. He was only about a hundred feet out from the American side when he sat down on the cable. Then he lay on his back, stood up on one foot, and then continued on his way. When he reached the middle of the river, the little steamer *Maid-of-the-Mist* floated underneath him. He dropped a cord to the deck, pulled up a bottle, drank from it, then continued toward Canada. Eighteen minutes after he had left the American side he had arrived on the Canadian as safely as though he had been merely out for a stroll in the park.

In the weeks that followed, Blondin varied his per-formance and the crowds continually grew in size. He walked across blindfolded. Another time he pushed a wheelbarrow. He walked across on stilts. He stood on his head over the middle of the gorge. He held out a hat to be perforated by a sharpshooter on the *Maid-of-the-Mist*. He walked at night, with colored lights on the ends of his balancing pole. He even carried his 145-pound manager across on his back, although he did stop and rest seven times along the way.

In 1860 Blondin returned to Niagara a world celebrity and repeated his previous performances. A few new touches were also added. Queen Victoria's 18-year-old son, who in later years would become King Edward VII, visited the falls that summer and was invited to take a ride across the gorge in Blondin's barrow. This extension of the itinerary was quickly vetoed by more mature members of the prince's entourage.

After his Niagara triumphs, Blondin toured extensively in North America and then made a circuit of the globe. In 1888, at the age of 64, he returned to America. When a scheme to use New York City's Central Park for his high-wire act fell through, Blondin terminated three weeks of performances on nearby Staten Island after only two weeks and returned to Europe.

On February 22, 1897, the famous Frenchman who had defied death on the high wire thousands of times, had logged approximately 10,000 miles on the high wire and had begun earning his fame and fortune at Niagara Falls in 1859, died in London, at the age of 73, in bed.

A REMARKABLE
LITTLE LADY

Only a few Americans have been honored by having their names perpetuated through association with articles of clothing. Wealthy and philanthropic Philadelphia hat manufacturer John B. Stetson joined this exclusive circle when his name became synonymous with the high-crowned, broad-brimmed head covering worn by Western cowboys for the past hundred years. The first name of San Francisco trouser tycoon Levi Strauss became just about as famous when these same cowboys adopted his tough, blue denim pants, their pockets reinforced with shiny copper rivets, many decades before faded blue jeans became a staple of the American wardrobe.

Both Stetson and Strauss grew accustomed to being known for their links with articles of clothing. But Amelia Jenks Bloomer, the temperance reformer, women's rights editor and suffragist, regretted her lasting connection with the strange-looking pants that bore her name.

When Amelia Jenks married Dexter Bloomer in 1840 the word "obey" was stricken from the bride's vows. Thus

43

began a marriage in which Mr. Bloomer respected his wife's autonomy to a then-shocking degree. The couple settled in Seneca Falls in New York's lovely Finger Lakes region. Dexter was coeditor of the *Seneca County Courier* and Amelia contributed articles to the paper on political and social topics. She also contributed to a local temperance publication, *The Water Bucket.*

In 1849 Amelia began publication of her own "monthly journal devoted to temperance and literature." It was called *The Lily,* and when its subject matter was expanded to include such topics as education, unjust marriage laws and women's rights, she spoke out on freedom of dress, defending specifically the wearing of "pantalettes" by an actress of her day, Fanny Kemble.

Amelia was probably the first American woman magazine editor. Then, when her husband gave up the newspaper to accept an appointment as postmaster of Seneca Falls, she became deputy postmaster, something also unheard of at the time. Next door to the post office she opened a reading room for the convenience of ladies whose fathers or husbands would not allow *The Lily* in the house.

Seneca Falls was a newsworthy town at this time. The celebrated women's rights convention had been held there in July 1848, under the leadership of Lucretia Mott and Elizabeth Cady Stanton. Amelia Bloomer had attended the convention as an interested spectator, and soon Mrs. Stanton became one of the contributors to *The Lily.*

One day one of Mrs. Stanton's acquaintances, Elizabeth Smith Miller, appeared in Seneca Falls wearing a costume she had designed for herself while traveling in Europe. It consisted of loose Turkish trousers gathered at the ankles, a skirt extending about halfway between the knee and ankle and a loose-fitting bodice. In the next issue of *The Lily,* Amelia Bloomer publicized this outfit and her name was quickly connected with the style although she did not create it. The "Bloomer costume" was made fun of and became a sign of radicalism. Mrs. Bloomer, Elizabeth Cady Stanton, Susan B. Anthony and other leaders of the women's rights movement wore the new garments.

Although the editors of most newspapers were horrified,

and said so, editor Bloomer's fan mail began to pile up. Her readers, intrigued with the thought of shucking the long, heavy skirts and multiple petticoats in vogue at the time, wrote many letters asking for information and patterns. Amelia answered their inquiries in the pages of *The Lily.* A picture of Mrs. Stanton and the editor wearing the new mode of dress appeared in one issue. The journal also attacked "tight lacing," a Victorian means of improving the female figure that did just the opposite to a girl's vital organs. Subscriptions to *The Lily* doubled almost overnight, and, by 1853, it had become a twice-a-month publication with a circulation of 6,000.

The cartoonists and humor magazines both in the United States and abroad found inspiration in the "Bloomer costume." During the 1851-52 season, three farces based on it were running on the London stage and one in Paris. Songwriters contributed "The Bloomer Waltz" and "The Bloomer Polka."

After a few years Mrs. Bloomer and her feminist friends stopped wearing bloomers when they realized that the notoriety surrounding dress reform was diverting attention from the real issues in their cause.

In 1854 Dexter Bloomer had an opportunity to return to the newspaper business, in Mount Vernon, Ohio. The couple moved there and took along the now flourishing *Lily,* which was printed in the same shop as Dexter's weekly paper. Not afraid to act on her own beliefs, Amelia hired a woman as a compositor for *The Lily* and retained her, despite a strike by her husband's male typesetters.

After two years in Ohio, Dexter decided he wanted to live on the frontier, in Council Bluffs, Iowa. While Amelia agreed to the move, it was decided that this time *The Lily* would have to remain behind. There were no facilities in Council Bluffs for printing and mailing such a thriving publication. It was sold to Mary B. Birdsall a less capable editor than the founder. A year later *The Lily* went out of business. In Council Bluffs, Amelia worked to establish churches and Good Templar lodges. She was active in relief work during the Civil War, and for the rest of her life remained an ardent disciple of change.

LINCOLN WANTED ONLY ONE WAR

People in positions of authority sometimes do seemingly strange things.

A prize example of this was Secretary of State William Henry Seward, who began his long cabinet career by placing on Abraham Lincoln's desk what noted historian Bruce Catton has called "as completely fantastic a note as any American President ever received from his Secretary of State."

Seward served as governor of New York and was twice elected to the United States Senate. He had confidently expected to receive the Republican presidential nomination in 1860, only to be passed over when the convention deadlocked and a compromise candidate, the comparatively unknown "railsplitter" from Illinois, was chosen. Appointed to the top cabinet post by the victorious Lincoln, Seward was to head the State Department with great distinction for eight years and win lasting fame for negotiating the purchase of Alaska from Russia for a mere $7,200,000.[1]

But on April 1, 1861, just twelve days before the first shot of the Civil War was fired at Fort Sumter in the harbor of Charleston, South Carolina, Seward presented Lincoln the amazing memorandum headed, "Some Thoughts for the President's Consideration." This note recommended that the United States become involved in a foreign war as the best means of averting strife between the North and South.

When Lincoln had been sworn in as President on March 4, 1861, seven Southern states had already seceded from the Union. Less than a month later, the new secretary was arguing that the way to get the seven states back into the family was to declare war on France and Spain, both of whom were believed to be meddling in the affairs of our neighbor Mexico. Seward also suggested to the President that we let Great Britain and Russia know that we would stand for no nonsense from either of them. Threatened by danger from without, Seward contended, the sections of the shattered nation would forget their differences and be pulled together by the common cause of foreign war.

Although Lincoln received Seward's proposal on April Fool's Day, he had no choice but to take the matter seriously. As President, he would have been well within his rights to ask for the resignation of his top cabinet officer. However, instead of censuring or dismissing Seward on the grounds of poor judgment, Lincoln patiently penned a reply to him explaining in detail why the recommendation could not be followed. Then, in characteristic fashion, he pigeonholed Seward's unique document and made sure it would not be made public until both statesmen had passed on. In all fairness to Seward, it should be noted that once he realized Lincoln meant to be "boss," he carried out his duties admirably and earned an enviable reputation as a diplomat.

Before 1861 was over, the foreign war that Seward had

[1]For the story of the purchase of Alaska read *Alaska Puzzle* on page 73.

been asking for was almost thrust upon the North.

On November 15, the *USS San Jacinto,* commanded by Captain Charles Wilkes, dropped anchor in Hampton Roads, Virginia. On board as prisoners were James Mason of Virginia and John Slidell of Louisiana, Confederate Commissioners to the governments of England and France, respectively. Acting on his own, Wilkes had stopped the British mail steamer *Trent* on its way from Havana, Cuba to Southampton, England and forcibly removed the two commissioners and their male secretaries. With the ordering of a warning shot to be fired across the *Trent's* bow, Wilkes had apparently forgotten that in 1812 the United States had gone to war primarily because of Britain's high-handed treatment of neutral shipping.

Throughout the North, Captain Wilkes was applauded heartily. Secretary of the Navy Gideon Welles wrote a letter of commendation and the House of Representatives voted its thanks. The city of Boston, where the impetuous captain eventually took his captives for safekeeping, staged a banquet in his honor. There was even talk there of presenting him with a sword.

Meanwhile, across the Atlantic, the Britishers were reacting angrily. Parliament and London's clubs resounded with war talk. The Union Jack had been insulted; amends must be made quickly, or else! Troops were immediately dispatched from England to Canada to bolster garrisons there. Queen Victoria's naval forces in the West Indies were also strengthened.

The Southern leaders were not displeased with this unexpected turn of events. This twisting of the British lion's tail by the Union navy could possibly lead to intervention by England in the Civil War, which would mean a strong ally for the Confederacy in its struggle with the North. Wishful thinkers south of the Potomac pictured Her Majesty's men-of-war sweeping the Yankee blockade ships from the seas and Southern ports again being open to a booming cotton trade.

Secretary Seward, notorious for his anti-British sentiments, was no doubt enjoying the furor, but he was cautious enough to let Charles Francis Adams, United

States Minister in London, know that Captain Wilkes had acted without authority or orders from Washington. Seward also asked Lincoln's new general of the army, George B. McClellan, what the chances were of continuing the fight against the Confederacy with one hand and taking on Great Britain with the other. Military man that he was, McClellan was properly pessimistic. He too preferred only one war at a time.

In this explosive atmosphere the British Cabinet drafted a harsh note for Queen Victoria's approval. Prince Albert, the Queen's consort, reviewed it and recommended a softening of the wording so that it would be easier for the Americans to come around and admit that Wilkes had stepped out of line.

Despite the clamor over Wilkes, the new national hero, Seward and Lincoln got the message. The President, who from the beginning had thought the United States had a rather poor case, was still strongly in favor of only one war at a time.

Although the pill was a bitter one to swallow, the cabinet decided, at a Christmas Day meeting in 1861, to turn the two internationally famous prisoners loose. The decision was announced in a masterly bit of diplomatic double-talk by Secretary Seward that stopped short of apology but, nevertheless, served to smooth things over. A Seward biographer, Dexter Perkins, wrote later: "He solved the difficulty by a great dispatch in which he showed that to yield to Great Britain in this case was to maintain the great American principle of freedom of the seas."

When one of Her Majesty's ships docked at Boston to pick up Mason and Slidell, the case was closed and there was many a sigh of relief on both sides of the Atlantic. Good relations between the North and Great Britain appeared to have been restored with amazing speed. Shortly after the conclusion of the Trent Affair, the British government, having an occasion to send troops to Canada, asked and was given permission to land them at Portland, Maine. From this point they could continue to their destination by rail and thus avoid the hardships of a wintry voyage up the St. Lawrence River.

49

MISSION FROM MUSCOVY

Attempting to figure out what the Russians are up to is an old, old game.

In the autumn of 1863, with America torn asunder by internal warfare, newspaper readers of both the North and South were astonished to read that six Russian warships had appeared in New York harbor. Within a few weeks the wonder grew as another man-of-war flying the ensign of Muscovy dropped anchor inside San Francisco's Golden Gate, to be followed at brief intervals by five more.

With the exception of urbane Edouard de Stoeckl, Czar Alexander II's veteran minister to Washington, and a Captain Crown who had arrived a few weeks earlier to inform Stoeckl, no one on this side of the Atlantic knew exactly what had prompted this sudden and unexpected appearance of a dozen Russian fighting ships in Northern harbors. This uncertainty made little difference to most Northerners, who interpreted the visit as a gesture of friendship toward the Union. Many even considered it a warning to Russia's enemies, France and England, to stay out of Uncle Sam's affairs, even though recent Union victories at Vicksburg and Gettysburg had dampened the ardor of these two European powers for recognizing the Confederacy. With the North taking this point of view, the Russians had no need to offer any explanation for their appearance.

The welcome given the surprise naval visitors was particularly enthusiastic in New York, where a Russian warship had never been seen before. British and French men-of-war frequently used the harbor, even during the Civil War. In fact, a squadron of each was at anchor there when, in late September of 1863, the first of the Russian vessels arrived. She was the steam frigate *Osliaba,* mounting 33 guns and manned by about 450 men.

Two days later *The New York Times* announced that other ships had been sighted and described in glowing terms a visit by some of its staff to the *Osliaba.*

. . . we found her officers in the best of spirits at the prospect of soon being joined by so large a force of their countrymen, with whom they can share the pleasures of their visit here, and the attentions that are about to be paid them by our citizens and the Municipal Government. . . The *Osliaba* has been absent from Russia for two years, and came to this port from Cadiz . . . . Those who have been on board of her all speak in the highest terms of her appearance and management, and of the rare intelligence and gentlemanly bearing of her officers of every grade. We were told by the courteous midshipman who escorted us through the frigate, that all officers belonging to the Russian navy are required to be able to speak English and French.

The elaborateness of the New York welcome was perhaps best reflected in the pages of *Harper's Weekly.* On October 17 this magazine devoted its entire front page to a woodcut of a reception for the Common Council on the deck of the frigate *Alexander Nevsky*, flagship of Admiral Stepan Lisovski. Inside was a full-page illustration of bearded Russian sailors parading on lower Broadway and a two-page spread depicting five Russian ships at anchor but with most of their sails up, probably for artistic reasons.

On the political side, *Harper's Weekly* carried a lengthy editorial questioning George Washington's famous warning against foreign entanglements and urging that the U.S. form an alliance with Russia.

In its issue of November 21, *Harper's Weekly* had room for little else besides the grand ball given the Russian officers at the New York Academy of Music on November 5. But there was one slightly sour note, which read: "Should this number of *Harper's Weekly* fall into the hands of some poor fellow wounded at Chattanooga or some half-starved Union prisoner in Richmond, the contrast between his own condition and that of the scented and perfumed dancers who figure in the ball picture may not improve his temper."

In San Francisco, where the Czar's warships were no novelty, two having paid a visit to the young metropolis of the West only a year before, the welcome for the Russians was less spectacular but no less enthusiastic. Here, too, Russian officers danced with society belles.

The Russian admiral, Alexander Popov, was so enthusiastic about his San Francisco reception he almost became involved in military action to defend the city. Upon hearing a rumor that Confederate sea-raiders were about to bombard the virtually defenseless seaport, he ordered his crews to strip for action. His grand gesture later earned him a stinging rebuke from his superiors back home in St. Petersburg who favored a more neutral attitude.

As New York and San Francisco rolled out the red carpet and the Secretary of the Navy, Gideon Welles, offered the facilities of the Brooklyn Navy Yard, the British watched with an astute eye. They quickly discerned the real reason the western hemisphere was unexpectedly being treated to a display of Russian naval strength. The simple truth was buried in the third paragraph of the following dispatch and is italicized here for emphasis. Written by an English journalist in New York, it appeared on October 20, 1863, in the *Bermuda Royal Gazette,* a weekly established in 1828 that is still published today.

The dispatch begins by describing an extremely colorful scene in New York harbor. Numbers following the names of the various British ships indicate the number of guns carried.

New York. Her Britannic Majesty's ship *Nile,* 78, Capt. E.K. Barnard, arrived at this port on Tuesday, from Halifax, bearing the flag of Rear Admiral Sir Alexander Milne, K.C.B., with the temporary rank of Vice-Admiral, who commands our squadron on what is officially termed the North America and West Indies station. With the *Nile* was her tender the *Nimble,* 5, Lieut. D'Arcy; and there came in at the same time, from Bermuda, the *Immortalite,* 35, Capt. Hancock. These three ships are anchored abreast of Governor's Island. . . .

On Tuesday, also, the French frigate *Guerriere,* flagship of Rear-Admiral Reynaud and returning from her late trip to Newfoundland and Nova Scotia, anchored in the North River, where were already lying three or four of her smaller consorts. The arrival of the Russian admiral's flagship, the *Alexander Nevsky,* has already been noticed; and as his squadron consists of five ships, the French of the same number, and the British of three, this unusual assemblage of men-of-war gives the river a very picturesque and animated appearance.

But the causes of the simultaneous muster have puzzled some of our excellent contemporaries, who must needs interpret very ordinary occurrences as big with portent. Yet the matter is very easily expounded, without diving deep into the secrets of state policy. Our worthy Admiral (British) has been, not unnaturally, attracted hither by a desire to see with his own eyes this great emporium of commerce, this metropolis of the Western world; and New York men are the very last who ought to wonder at such legitimate curiosity.—*The Russian ships, as we stated a week ago, were unquestionably ordered hither as to the most eligible and desirable of neutral ports, pending the differences between the Czar and the western powers of Europe.*—The frequent presence of French vessels is, one would suppose, sufficiently explained by the French occupation of Mexico, which entails much naval service in an unhealthy climate and therefore renders change desirable for crews. In addition to this, the necessity for sending down supplies, and for transmitting dispatches that arrive here from France by the Liverpool steamers, is too obvious to be missed. In short, and notwithstanding the somewhat complicated relations of the United States with several European states, only those Editors who are accustomed to extract sunbeams from cucumbers can deduce any political significance from this chance meeting in these waters.

On the other hand, it was only in the due course of events that the Russian visitors should meet with a most cordial reception. It could not be otherwise. The American national mind is possessed with the idea that perfect accord exists, in this case, between the Democracy of the New World and the Autocracy of the Old. Wrapt in the delusions of national vanity, our good cousins here mistake the policy of Russia, in cultivating a close alliance with them, for a profound admiration of their system of Government. And they have repeated this to themselves so often, that there is no disenchanting them.

To the writer of the foregoing dispatch, the reasons behind the Russian move were very obvious. And he was quite right. In sending her naval squadrons to American waters Russia was simply protecting her own interests. A decade earlier, during the Crimean War, her Baltic fleet had been rendered completely ineffective by the enemy who confined the fleet to the harbor of Kronstadt in the Gulf of Finland. Now, in 1863, the oppressed people of Poland were rebelling against their Muscovite masters, and Anglo-French intervention on behalf of the Poles seemed imminent. Therefore, the Czar's ships had taken shelter in the harbors of a friendly, neutral power to prevent their being trapped a second time should Europe take up arms once more.

Furthermore, even though Russia's ships were wooden and depended largely on sail power, her optimistic Minister of Marine believed that when based in neutral ports they would, should war break out, be in a favorable position to raid England's seaborne commerce. If

Northerners of 1863 derived comfort from the naive thought that their newfound friends were capable of standing up to the more modern British navy, why should the visiting Russians disillusion them? Admirals Lisovski in New York and Popov in San Francisco simply looked wise and listened attentively to all the talk about America's admiration for things Russian.

After several months of New York's attentions, which included a visit to Niagara Falls for a group of Russian officers, the Atlantic squadron left for Washington, arriving there in early December. Anchored at Alexandria, the warships flying a strange flag drew crowds of capital residents, who boarded excursion steamers at the Seventh Street Wharf for trips around the fleet. Secretaries William H. Seward and Gideon Welles entertained the officers, as did Russian Minister Stoeckl and his Massachusetts-born wife, the former Eliza Howard. President Lincoln, who had returned in poor health from the dedication of Gettysburg National Cemetery, was unable to attend any of the functions.

A few months later Europe settled its differences over the Poles without resorting to arms. Lisovski's command split up and followed orders from the Minister of Marine to scrutinize some of John Bull's colonial possessions.

For example, the corvette *Variag,* mounting 17 guns, spent more than a month in Bermuda. In spite of Mother England's antagonism toward Russia, the inhabitants of the island also appear to have been captivated by the charm of the visitors from overseas. On April 9 the *Bermuda Royal Gazette* had these glowing words for them: "Capt. Lundh and his officers have made themselves universal favorites and will be parted with regret on all sides when they leave."

Before returning to the Baltic, Admiral Lisovski stopped off in Boston for one more banquet and a taste of the oratory of Edward Everett, who had shared the speaker's platform with Lincoln at the Gettysburg dedication. Several of Admiral Popov's ships remained in San Francisco until mid-summer as he, too, was in no hurry to haul anchor and rush home.

CONFEDERATES SOUTH OF THE BORDER

More than 8,000 Southerners migrated to Latin America at the close of the Civil War in 1865. These exiles were from every level of society—generals and privates who refused to surrender, state governors and other Confederate officials who feared Union reprisals, and ordinary folk who could not face the conquering Yankees.

Most went to the Republic of Mexico, where they found considerable internal turmoil. The United States recognized Benito Juárez, a Zapotec Indian, as President. However, the machinery of government throughout most of the country was actually under the control of the troops of Napoleon III of France. A would-be empire builder, this nephew of the great Napoleon I had taken advantage of the American Civil War to gain a foothold in the western hemisphere. He connived with the political opponents of Juárez and placed a handsome Austrian archduke, who called himself Emperor Maximilian, on the throne in Mexico City—a throne often described as being propped up by

French bayonets. Sharing Maximilian's precarious position was his beautiful Empress, Carlota, the daughter of King Leopold I of Belgium.

While preoccupied with its own Civil War, the United States had been unable to apply the Monroe Doctrine. As a result, Napoleon and Maximilian openly disregarded the doctrine's nonintervention clause. After the war, Washington's diplomatic pressure on the French was increased and large quantities of gunpowder, lead and other military supplies for Juárez began crossing the Rio Grande from the north.

The largest group of Southerners to enter Mexico was a military unit, a remnant of a cavalry outfit known as the Missouri Iron Brigade which was led by colorful 35-year-old General Joseph O. Shelby. Famous for his daring raids in Arkansas and Missouri, Shelby was one of the few Confederate generals who never surrendered to the Union. There is no reliable figure on the number of men who went to Mexico with him. Estimates of his fighting strength vary widely, from several hundred to several thousand. In addition to his seasoned troopers, he was accompanied by a number of other high ranking officers and several state governors who joined him shortly before he crossed the border at Eagle Pass, Texas. On July 4, 1865, Shelby's men wrapped the Confederate battle flag, the Stars and Bars, around a rock and ceremoniously dropped it into the Rio Grande.

Although claiming neutrality, this body of mounted men, with supply wagons and artillery, actually was proceeding to Mexico City to offer its services to Maximilian. Their journey south was complicated by the concentration of Juaristas in the northern part of the country who doubted Shelby's avowed neutrality. The French had misgivings, too, on learning that Shelby had sold his heaviest guns to the Juaristas to raise much-needed cash, as well as to get rid of the cumbersome equipment.

Before reaching the first French outpost at Monterrey, the little Confederate army was attacked several times by guerillas. In an ambush while crossing the Salinas River, twenty-seven of Shelby's cavalrymen were killed and even more were wounded. Additional blood was shed, this time mostly by Mexican citizens, when two dozen Shelby men took it on themselves to rescue a beautiful young American girl allegedly held prisoner by a powerful landowner. Then, once inside the region under French control, there was constant harassment by French commanders, who considered the advancing Confederates interlopers rather than potential allies.

Finally, after more than a month amid the sand and cactus of northern Mexico, the survivors of the expedition arrived in the capital, Mexico City. On August 16 the emperor granted Shelby an audience at which the latter was informed that his Iron Brigade was not welcome as a fighting unit. Maximilian said, however, that he was happy to have the men as individuals and that plans were being made to locate them in agricultural colonies. To fiery young Southerners used to the smoke and din of battle, this was bad news. The group disintegrated. Some enlisted in the French forces, some joined the forces of Juárez and others went hunting for gold. Only a small group waited in Mexico City for Maximilian to donate the land for colonization.

Maximilian allowed Shelby to take over a hacienda of an exiled Mexican politican in October of 1865. After sending for his wife and two sons, he made his way to the plantation located in Cordoba, one of the numerous colonies set up for Confederate exiles, about 100 miles west of Vera Cruz. He also entered the freighting business, hauling supplies for the French army. But it was all in vain. In the spring of 1866, yielding to increasing pressure from Washington, Napoleon began withdrawing his troops. This was a signal for guerillas and the Indians whose land had been expropriated for the colonies by Maximilian to close in on the hapless settlers. Many Confederates soon realized the hopelessness of the situation and began drifting back to their homes in the southern United States.

A year later, Maximilian was captured by troops of the Republic of Mexico. Requests from people around the world to free Maximilian had no effect on Juárez. The rifles of a firing squad ended the emperor's life and the dreams of his few remaining imperialist supporters. Empress Carlota had returned to Europe earlier in a vain attempt to seek help for her husband. After learning of his death she became hopelessly insane. She spent her last sixty years at the family palace of Miramar near Trieste.

Confederate Shelby, ironically, was rescued by a U.S. gunboat sent into the Caribbean to protect Americans after the fall of Maximilian. After returning to the States he settled in Missouri, where he farmed and engaged in various largely unsuccessful business ventures, including operation of a coal mine. In 1876, now forty-five but still a romantic, he telegraphed President Ulysses S. Grant offering to raise a 1,000-man fighting unit to avenge the death of George Armstrong Custer and five troops of the Seventh Cavalry at the battle of the Little Big Horn.

Shelby consistently resisted any attempt to obtain political office on the strength of his military reputation. However, in 1893, he was appointed U.S. Marshal for Western Missouri by President Grover Cleveland. He held the office until his death in 1897 at the age of sixty-seven.

In 1865 Wilmer McLean, owner of a small farmhouse in Appomattox Court House, Virginia, became famous when Lee and Grant met in his living room to end the Civil War.

McLean tried to capitalize, without success however, on his prominence by selling photographs of his home, now known as "Surrender House." In 1891 M.E. Dunlap of Niagara Falls, New York, bought the house and from time to time announced promotion schemes involving visitation to the historic building. Finally, Dunlap had the house dismantled, saying it would be reassembled in Washington D.C. as a war museum. Nothing happened with these plans except that the house soon disappeared as souvenir hunters carried it away—brick by brick. Therefore it was necessary for the National Park Service to build a replica of the McLean house on the original site in 1949.

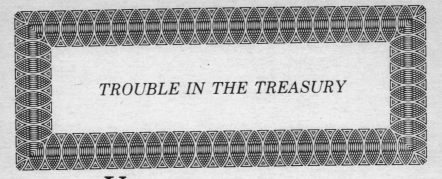

You never see the likeness of a living person on a U.S. postage stamp or paper bill, and for a very good reason. More than a century ago, Americans were surprised to see three of their contemporaries on U. S. currency. Congress objected to this form of personal advertising and made the practice illegal.

The congressional displeasure was expressed within the enactment commonly referred to as the Deficiency Appropriation Act of April 7, 1866. This act allocated funds for numerous government projects. One item reimbursed Brigham Young for $38,487.53 that the Mormon leader had advanced the government to straighten out Indian affairs in Utah. Another authorized payment of a $6,000 fuel bill for the White House and the Capitol. Sandwiched between these items was this brief paragraph covering considerably more than met the eye:

For plates, engraving, printing, and paper for national currency notes, two hundred and fifty thousand dollars: *Provided,* That no portrait or likeness of any living person hereafter engraved shall be placed upon any of the bonds, securities, notes, fractional or postal currency of the United States.

Up until the Civil War, day-to-day small business transactions were carried on largely with coins. The banks no longer redeemed paper money for coins beginning in December of 1861. This resulted in an increase in the value of coins, which encouraged hoarding. As the supply of coins dwindled, merchants and their customers found it impossible to conduct business. To remedy this intolerable situation, in 1862 Congress authorized the issuance of fractional currency, i.e., paper money in denominations of less than one dollar.

The first issue (1862), in denominations of 5-, 10-, 25-, and 50-cent notes, is known to collectors as Postage Currency, because the bills carried reproductions of postage stamps of the period, which had busts of George Washington and Thomas Jefferson. The design for the 50-cent note, for example, consisted chiefly of a row of five 10-cent Washington stamps.

The second issue (1863) looked more like the money we use today. Washington's picture appeared on all notes.

The third issue, which began circulating at the end of 1864, provided the impetus for the regulatory legislation. Washington still appeared on the 10-cent note and also on a new three-cent note which was issued to facilitate purchase of three-cent stamps. The controversy arose over the remaining notes of the third issue. The 50-cent note carried the likeness of General Francis E. Spinner, Treasurer of the United States, and the two-bit note showed William Pitt Fessenden, a prominent politician from Maine who had been Secretary of the Treasury, and thus Spinner's boss, since June of 1864.

The focal point of the "living persons" issue was the new 5-cent note that was adorned with a bearded face that few citizens recognized. The portrait was that of Spencer M. Clark, Superintendent of the National Currency Bureau, a subdivision of the Treasury Department which handled transactions with the private bank note companies that printed the paper money.

The actual circumstances that led to the use of Clark's portrait on the note are still a mystery. One source reports that Clark was ordered to use his portrait against his wishes. Another source claims that the portrait of Freeman Clarke, the Comptroller of the Currency, was designated to be used, but a misunderstanding resulted in the use of Spencer Clark's portrait. A third theory cites William Clark, the explorer of Lewis and Clark fame, as the person intended to be commemorated on the note.

Eventually the controversial matter was disposed of very neatly in the 1866 Deficiency Appropriation Act, as quoted above. Representative M. Russell Thayer of Pennsylvania, who authored the pertinent paragraph barring such shenanigans in the future, submitted it with this restrained comment: "I have nothing to say against that gentleman (Clark) and no reflection to cast upon him . . . . but I would like any man to tell me why his face should be on the money of the United States."

As Mr. Clark's notability was being questioned by Representative Thayer, two Civil War military heroes were caught in the barrage. A 15-cent note adorned with portraits of Ulysses S. Grant and William Tecumseh Sherman had reached what currency. fanciers call the specimen stage. As a result of the furor over the "living persons" issue, the faces of these famous generals never got into general circulation.

THE COLLINS
OVERLAND TELEGRAPH

Perry McDonough Collins
was the loser in one of the
greatest contests in the history of
communications—a thrilling
race to link the Old World and
the New by telegraph.

A famous figure in his day a
bit more than a century ago, his
name a household word, one
might say, in New York financial circles and around the
Department of State
in Washington,
Collins lost out to
Cyrus W. Field and
his Atlantic cable.
As a consequence,
many people have
never heard of him.
Nor will they find
his name in the
history books,
in *Who Was
Who in America,* or in any other standard biographical
reference work. Such seems to be the penalty for coming in
second, no matter how hard one tries.

Collins was an upstate New Yorker who migrated to California during the gold rush of 1849 and became involved in politics and business, including part ownership of a 60-mile-long telegraph line from Stockton east to the mines near Sonora. Like other prominent Californians of his time, he became intrigued with the potential of American trade with Siberian Russia. To see for himself, he made two trips to the empire of the czars, under Department of State auspices. The first (1856-57), which included the unprecedented feat, for an outsider, of traveling the full breadth of Siberia by sleigh and wagon, he narrated in reports to Washington, later elaborated on in a fascinating book, *A Voyage Down the Amoor, With a Land Journey Through Siberia.*

Rather oddly, the first edition of the book contains nothing about the grand telegraph scheme that was to make Perry McDonough Collins noteworthy. It was during his second visit to Russia, in 1859, that he conceived the daring idea of linking San Francisco and Europe with a telegraph line following the West Coast north to Bering Strait, where a relatively short stretch of underwater cable would connect Alaska with the Asiatic side, then continue across Siberia to European Russia and the capitals of the Old World.

Official Washington was enthusiastic about the Collins plan, as was the Western Union Company, especially since Cyrus W. Field's first attempt at installing an Atlantic cable had failed in 1858. There was no telegraph service west of Omaha, Nebraska, but in the fall of 1860, encouraged by a government subsidy, Western Union began planning to extend its wires to San Francisco. Then in the following spring came the attack on Fort Sumter, South Carolina, and the start of the Civil War.

California was too important to the Union to be joined to the East only by the Pony Express. At that time it took eight or nine days for a letter from St. Joseph, Missouri, to reach Sacramento, California. Accordingly, the telegraph line from Omaha to San Francisco was rushed to completion by October of 1861, in the process eliminating the Pony Express and bankrupting its promoters. Plans for the

Collins Overland Extension, however, were shelved temporarily because of the war. Despite the conflict, Western Union completed a line from San Francisco north to New Westminster, British Columbia, early in 1865.

Soon after the surrender at Appomattox in the spring of 1865, the telegraph again became big news. Cyrus Field went back to raising money for another attempt at laying some 2,000 miles of wire on the bottom of the Atlantic. Western Union president Hiram Sibley, who doubted that his competitor Field would ever succeed, plunged into the formidable task of making the Collins dream come true— setting poles and stringing wires through mountains and forests of British Columbia, Alaska (then known as Russian America), and eastern Siberia, much of the way through unexplored country.

Sibley had already bought concessions which Collins had negotiated with the U.S., British, and Russian governments and had made Collins a Western Union director. To finance the overland telegraph project Sibley organized a separate entity, the Western Union Extension Company, whose shares were offered to and quickly snapped up by Western Union stockholders.

By 1865 the Russians, impressed by the optimistic picture which Collins painted, but also in need of internal communications regardless of what happened in America, had installed "talking wires" for about three-quarters of the 7,000 miles from St. Petersburg, their capital, to Nikolaivsky on the eastern coast of Siberia at the mouth of the Amur River. This was encouraging, but there was still a herculean task facing the Americans.

Western Union decided to start operations at several points simultaneously. In the autumn of 1865 one party began work at the mouth of the Fraser River where the Canadian city of Vancouver, British Columbia now stands. A second established its base in Norton Sound, Alaska, just south of Bering Strait. A third crew landed at the mouth of the Anadyr River on the Asiatic side of Bering Strait (and promptly had its ship crushed in the ice, although food and construction materials were salvaged). All told, the project involved hundreds of men, among them scientists, explorers, telegraph technicians and engineers. An entire fleet of ships and thousands of tons of supplies and equipment were employed to construct the Collins Overland Line.

These crews worked diligently, surveying routes, cutting poles, and in British Columbia actually stringing wire. The hardships endured by the men Western Union sent to build the overland telegraph line included camping out in harsh, sub-freezing temperatures day after seemingly endless day. Digging holes in the frozen earth to receive the telegraph poles was slow, backbreaking work. Tools were continually broken by the rock-hard frozen soil. Frostbite and scurvy were constant scourges.

Then came the bombshell. At the end of July 1866, the last coils of Cyrus Field's new Atlantic cable unreeled from the hold of the largest ship in the world, the *Great Eastern,* in a fifth desperate attempt to lay the submarine telegraph line. The cable was brought safely ashore in Newfoundland and worked perfectly. Shortly afterward another cable, one that had broken at sea, was recovered and put into working order. When word of this got through to Sibley's surveying and construction crews hacking their way through the wilds of British Columbia and Alaska, they suffered bitter disappointment. Some of the men wept in utter frustration. Their project no longer was vital.

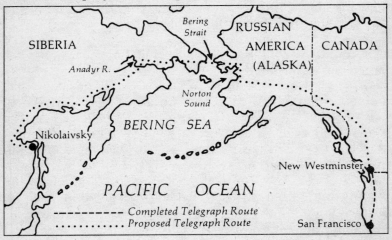

For a time Western Union put up a bold front and maintained the fiction that work was continuing on the Collins Overland Line. The white flag was run up officially on March 25, 1867, in a letter from Western Union vice president William Orton informing Secretary of State William H. Seward, an enthusiastic backer of the project, that the work of construction on the Collins Overland Line, after an expenditure of $3,000,000, had been discontinued.

It was not until a month later that the bad news got through to the isolated American crew on the Siberian side of the Pacific. A passing American whaling captain told them of the success of the new Atlantic cable and showed them San Francisco newspaper accounts. Accordingly, like their fellow workers on the American side, they packed up and came home. The *San Francisco Bulletin* for October 8, 1867, wrote the final chapter to the whole sad story with a lengthy dispatch beginning:

The Western Union Telegraph Company have completed the withdrawal of the men and material from Russian America and left their partially constructed line to the mercy of the elements and the good will of the Indians. The ships *Clara Bell* and *Nightingale* have arrived here within a few hours of each other, bringing with them 135 men and officers belonging to the construction party. Some of those who returned to San Francisco have been absent from civilization for two years and four months.

Thus ended the dream of Perry McDonough Collins. However, he actually fared well financially and, in addition to his book, managed to leave a monument or two to himself after all. Western Union had paid him $100,000 cash for his concessions. He invested this wisely in railroad securities and became a wealthy man. Upon his death in 1900 at the age of 87, he left the bulk of his estate to an unmarried niece. She in turn, in accordance with her uncle's wishes, left the sum of $1,500,000 to be divided among New York University, Columbia University and New York's Presbyterian Hospital.

67

BRIDES FOR SEATTLE

In the 1860's the fledgling town of Seattle, Washington Territory, like most frontier communities, suffered from a scarcity of unattached women. What Seattle did have was a very enterprising young man named Asa Mercer. His life was a series of diverse careers and adventures, including the honor of being the first president of the territorial university (which later became the University of Washington). This undoubtedly was related to the fact that the 22-year-old Mercer was the only college graduate for miles around.

After his experience at the university, Mercer addressed himself to the sad imbalance in Seattle's population, thus launching his most ambitious project ever. Taking into account the rate of male attrition on the East Coast because of the Civil War, he set off for New England, hoping to interest some well-bred unmarried or widowed ladies in a five-month journey to Puget Sound to meet prospective husbands. He succeeded in gathering about 12 adventurous women to make the trip. When word traveled that

68

these lovely immigrants had disembarked on May 16, 1864, bachelors of the struggling outpost on Puget Sound lost no time in introducing themselves. Before long the women had settled down in their new environment, some as wives and others as schoolteachers.

Now Seattle's hero, Mercer decided to try again, this time on a larger scale. He would go directly to President Lincoln, request a government vessel, and bring out hundreds of women left alone by the war. Many a lonesome miner or logger eagerly contributed $300 to Mercer's travel expense fund in the hope of obtaining a spouse.

On his second trip east Mercer arrived at New York on the very day President Lincoln was assassinated. With the national capital in turmoil, he spent a few months in New England working on his scheme. Then, backed by Gov. John Andrew of Massachusetts, he tackled Washington's bureaucracy, with frustrating results.

However, somewhere along the way Mercer received enough encouragement to announce, in a circular dated September 8, 1865, that widows and orphan daughters of slain Union soldiers were invited to sail with him in about two weeks. The cost of their passage would range from $125 to $150. There was no mention of the true purpose behind the expedition, only a vague statement that the citizens of Washington Territory guaranteed employment to all women of good character who would go along. Families were invited to go along, too, with children traveling at half-fare. Unattached men were unwelcome.

While many newspapers ignored or ridiculed Mercer's project, *The New York Times* gave it enthusiastic support. Its issue for September 30 carried two full columns about Mercer, concluding with the welcome news that a steamer, the 235-foot-long *Continental,* had been promised by the government and would sail shortly with 700 happy women aboard. But somehow the *Continental* was sold to a private company for service on the West Coast. Rather than give up, Mercer made a deal with the new owners for passage as far as San Francisco, the ship's destination.

EMIGRATION TO WASHINGTON TERRITORY OF 400 WOMEN ON THE STEAMER *CONTINENTAL* was the caption under a two-page picture spread in *Harper's Weekly* magazine on January 6, 1866. Delightful sketches showed the heavily loaded vessel leaving her birth in New York harbor with a crowd of attractive female passengers, dressed in the height of fashion, on board.

While all this probably was taken as gospel by *Harper's* readers in Boston and Philadelphia, New Yorkers knew better. On January 6, 1866, the *Continental* was still tied fast to her dock, as additional delays and the cost of New York hotel rooms thinned the ranks of the potential *émigrés*. But the whistle finally blew. On January 16 the *Continental* headed for sea with Mercer and his surviving candidates for matrimony. The passenger list totaled just over one hundred. Except for four people going only as far as Rio de Janeiro, Brazil, all were considered members of the Mercer party. A number of family groups were included and, in spite of Mercer's earlier attempt to discourage them, a few unattached single men were aboard.

For some unaccountable reason, several women were left behind. When these entered suit against Mercer and the steamship company, *The Times* cooled off on the great organizer. It criticized him on its editorial page and gave detailed coverage of the lawsuits. But when a young *Times* reporter, Roger Conant, who had accompanied the expedition, began sending back exciting accounts of the girls' adventures, readers were treated to many columns of interesting dispatches datelined Rio de Janeiro, Brazil, and Lota, Chile.

In addition to writing for *The Times* about the *Continental*'s voyage, Roger Conant kept a diary in which he recorded many human interest stories of a somewhat personal nature that never got into his newspaper stories. His diary was published in 1960 by the University of Washington Press under the title *Mercer's Belles, The Journal of a Reporter,* edited by Lenna A. Deutsch. The following excerpt is the account of his introduction to some fellow passengers. (Conant uses the editorial "we.")

Jan. 20th. During the past three days our time has been entirely occupied in taking care of the sea sick virgins . . . .

Yesterday while holding the head of a young virgin, the ship gave a sudden lurch. In order to save our self, we grasped at some thing, we knew not at the moment what and lo! it was the waist of the unfortunate virgin. In another second we were lying on the opposite side of the state room, with her in our arms. As she was in her night dress, her feelings must have been anything but pleasant. We looked at each other for half a minute, inexpressible astonishment depicted in our faces. We were called to a realizing sense of our situation, by a young lady from an upper berth, exclaiming "You great Muggins why don't you put her back in the berth?". . .

This afternoon while walking the port side of the ship, a young and interesting virgin suddenly exclaimed "Oh, Mr. Conant!" We at once rushed to her side and tenderly inquired as to the state of her health. She said nothing, but placed her hands across her stomach in an impressive manner. We instantly seized her by the arm pits, and hurrying her to the railing, held her there while she cast her bread upon the waters . . . .While going down the saloon, one of the state room doors flew violently open, and a very sea sick virgin was thrown from her berth directly across our path. "This is rather an abrupt introduction," we said in a sympathizing voice, "and is what may be called the free and easy style, but if you have no objection we will assist you to your berth." She made no reply, but springing to her feet like a kitten rushed into her state room and slammed the door after her.

Both in dispatches and in the diary Conant indicates that, except for some embarrassing episodes like those described above, most of the women thoroughly enjoyed the adventure. There was a piano on board the ship and several of the women were able to provide musical diversion for the passengers and crew. Roger Conant's diary relates an unfortunate incident vis-à-vis this piano:

Tuesday, Jan. 23rd. Piano which has had full sway of the fore part of the upper saloon, was set upon its legs this morning much to the relief of some of the anxious Mothers and more particularly to the old Doctor (Charles Barnard), who yesterday received a severe shock of the bowels, which proved not at all pleasant to a man of his sensitive organization. He was making an eloquent

71

speech to some of the ladies, when the steamer gave one of those unfortunate lurches for which she is celebrated, and prostrated the Dr. full length over the piano. It was not known at first which was most injured by the collision. But as the Doctor soon recovered, while the piano was out of tune for the rest of the voyage, I concluded that of the two, the Doctor's stomach had proved the strongest. We have music now from the rising of the sun to the going down thereof.

The weather was beautiful throughout the trip, and no one was taken ill with anything more serious than seasickness. Several times the ship was overrun by dashing Chilean army officers who would have carried off some of the passengers were it not for the alertness of Mr. Mercer. Once, at the port of Lota, an attempt at girl-napping seemed so imminent that Mercer had to take his stand at the gangway, with pistol drawn.

Another tense moment of the voyage came when the captain of the *Continental* steered into Coronel, Chile, thinking it was Lota and not realizing it was blockaded by the Spanish navy. Upon emerging from the harbor he was stopped by warning shots from a warship. Some of his female passengers fainted; others wept as they pictured themselves thrown into Spanish dungeons. The boarding party fortunately found the steamer's papers in good order and the incident ended with a handshake.

The *Continental* steamed through the Golden Gate on April 24, 1866, fourteen weeks after sailing. About thirty-six passengers elected to stay in San Francisco, which had its own quota of lonely bachelors not above trying to convince the women that Seattle was a horrible place to live. Asa Mercer divided the remainder of his charges into small groups and, via lumber vessels returning empty to Puget Sound, managed to deliver them to their intended destination. Two of the women who stayed in San Francisco and several of those who went to Seattle married members of the *Continental's* crew, which seemed to defeat Mercer's purpose in promoting the migration. One of the women, Annie Stephens of Baltimore, married Asa Mercer in Seattle's Methodist Church in July 1866.

ALASKA PUZZLE

In 1967 Alaska celebrated the centennial of its acquisition by the United States. Although many years have passed since Russia sold us the future forty-ninth state, one question remains unanswered—did certain Congressmen vote for the unpopular purchase only after taking money from the Russian minister?

There was much more involved than a mere real estate transaction, albeit a huge one, when Secretary of State Seward and Russian minister Stoeckl put their signatures on the Alaska Purchase Treaty at 4 a.m. on March 30, 1867. There would be little exaggeration in saying they exploded a bomb under Washington. When the smoke had cleared, two years later, here is how the picture looked: First, the Stars and Stripes flew over a wilderness more than twice the size of Texas, obtained at the bargain rate of about two cents an acre, half the per-acre price paid to Napoleon for the vast Louisiana Territory. Second, the reputations of a number of prominent Washingtonians were somewhat tarnished. Third, Russian Minister Stoeckl, along with his Massachusetts-born wife, until then a popular couple in Capital society, had said "good-bye forever" to America, with the country saying "good riddance."

Edouard de Stoeckl, who like to be called "Baron" although there is no evidence that he was of noble birth, had served his country in Washington for 28 years. As an urbane bachelor of 33, he had come to the United States in 1841 to join the legation staff headed by Minister Alexander Bodisco, a 62-year-old widower who shortly thereafter provided the Capital with interesting small talk by marrying the teenage daughter of a clerk in the Adjutant General's office and in due course fathering seven children by his new wife.

In January 1854, just after the start of the Crimean War in which Russia eventually was defeated by France, England, Sardinia and Turkey, Minister Bodisco was killed in Washington by a fall from his horse and Stoeckl became top man at the legation with the title chargé d'affaires. Two years later, with the blessing of Czar Alexander II, he married Eliza Howard, youngest daughter of John Howard of Springfield, Massachusetts, whom he met while she was visiting a married sister living in Washington. In 1857 Stoeckl was appointed minister.

As early as the Crimean War, Stoeckl had initiated talks about the possible sale of Alaska with influential and energetic Senator William Gwin of California, a man in a better position than most Easterners to evaluate the region's untapped resources. However, nothing happened. It seems to have been a personal project with Stoeckl in which his government had little interest at the time. Nevertheless, his dispatches to Russia continued to hint at Alaska's vulnerability and the desirability of getting rid of it.

In 1860, through the influence of the Czar's brother, Grand Duke Constantine, who was extremely hostile toward the Russian-American Company which held the government monopoly for developing and extracting Alaska's resources, Russia began to favor parting with her distant possession. Stoeckl reopened the subject with Gwin, who had the ear of President James Buchanan. But

74

in the fall of that year Lincoln was elected. North and South soon were plunged into bitter civil war. Alaska was forgotten. Forgotten, that is, by almost everyone in Washington but the Russian minister, who clung tenaciously to the idea that he would be doing his own government a great favor by getting rid of her frozen wastes in the western hemisphere.

Shortly after peace had once more returned to America, Stoeckl visited St. Petersburg, then Russia's capital, and gave his opinion that the chances of a United States purchase of Alaska were good. Actually, nobody of any importance in Washington except Secretary of State William H. Seward, an avowed expansionist, had the slightest interest. California's Gwin, whose sympathies had been with the South, had fled to Europe after having been locked up for eight months in Fort Jackson, Louisiana, with no charges preferred against him. Presumably he had conspired with Napoleon III to take over Mexico's mineral-rich state of Sonora while the United States was occupied with its Civil War.

Czar Alexander II, Foreign Minister Gortchakov and other highly-placed Russians had grown tired of hearing about their faraway possession that was benefiting the mother country not one whit. At the time of Stoeckl's postwar visit the Russian-American Company was in financial trouble and had become a drain on the Russian treasury. So Stoeckl suddenly was instructed to negotiate a sale.

Secretary Seward soon heard that Alaska was on the market. With the reluctant approval of President Andrew Johnson and the Cabinet members, all of whom were sworn to secrecy, Seward offered $5 million. Stoeckl wanted more. Within a few days, through the magic of the new Atlantic cable, Stoeckl was authorized to compromise. He and Seward arrived at a figure of $7,200,000. On the evening of March 29, 1867, Stoeckl called on Seward at the latter's home with the news that his government was agreeable to the price and to a draft of a treaty that had been cabled to Russia, at U.S. expense.

Seward had not a moment to lose. Not even the President could contract for such a large parcel of real estate without the approval of Congress, and Congress was about to adjourn. Although the hour was late, Seward asked Stoeckl to round up his staff and meet him at the State Department. He immediately sent for Massachusetts Senator Charles Sumner, chairman of the Senate Foreign Relations Committee, who had been opposed to buying Alaska but had been won over by Seward to his cause. Several State Department clerks were routed out of bed. By 4 o'clock on the morning of March 30 a final draft of the treaty was signed and sealed. That same day the document was presented to an astonished Senate, whose consent, by a two-thirds majority, was necessary.

With the Northern radicals in control of Congress and sentiment against Johnson's reconstruction policies building up to the point where it soon would culminate in the unprecedented impeachment of a President, many senators were loathe to go along with the Administration on anything. And who cared anyway about Alaska, that outlandish abode of Eskimos and seals? But strangely enough, after days of heated discussion along with tireless personal lobbying by Secretary Seward, Senator Sumner put the proposal across with a masterful three-hour oration describing the region's potential resources in great detail and stressing the strong friendship that existed between Russia and the United States during the late war.

No one could deny that throughout the Civil War Russia's sympathies, as contrasted with those of France and England, had been with the North. The senators also remembered that in the fall of 1863 Union morale had been given a boost by the visit of friendly Russian warships to New York and San Francisco.[1]

The truth of the matter was that the Russians were not making a gesture of friendship. Europe appeared to be about to go to war over Russia's treatment of the Poles. In the event of actual hostilities, Russia's navy probably would have been bottled up by the British fleet as had hap-

[1]For a more complete version of this misunderstanding, see *Mission from Muscovy* on page 50.

pened during the Crimean War. Therefore the Russian high command was taking no chances. They wished to base their ships in neutral ports so that her men-of-war would at least be in a position to raid British and French seaborne commerce.

But the senators considering the Alaska Purchase Treaty weren't aware of this. They knew only that in the Union's time of trial the Russians had been considered our steadfast friends. Thus what historians later labelled "the myth of Russian-American friendship" worked strongly in favor of Seward's proposal that we oblige Russia by taking up her offer to sell her far-distant outpost. When the vote on the treaty was taken, on April 9, 1867, twenty-seven out of thirty-nine senators present voted in the affirmative. This was just one more than needed to approve the treaty. Ignoring a plea for unanimity, two members still held out, and the vote of record stands at thirty-seven to two.

An editorial in *Harper's Weekly* four days after the treaty was signed probably was representative of public sentiment at the time:

A more inopportune moment than this for the territorial expansion of the United States could not have been found... It is our "manifest destiny" ultimately to rule the continent, but that is no reason why we should immediately annex Mexico, or make war upon Canada, or buy Russian America. Before we enlarge our borders let us thoroughly organize our present possessions.

Two weeks later, in an editorial headed "The New National Ice-House," *Harper's* criticized Seward for the secrecy surrounding the negotiations and ended by predicting a bleak future for Alaska.

The House of Representatives still had to appropriate the money for Alaska. The House wanted no part of the future forty-ninth state at any price, and adjourned for spring recess without even considering a bill. Indeed, it was May of 1868, more than a year later, before the matter ever got to the floor. There was no lack of discussion in committees and in the press, however. Much of it was unfavorable to Seward and the bold project that was to earn him his most lasting fame. "Seward's Folly," "Seward's Icebox," "Walrussia" and "Icebergia" were among the uncomplimentary terms applied to the northern land that later was to return its purchase price more than a hundredfold in minerals alone, not to mention countless valuable furs, forest products, salmon and those giant crabs with the tasty king-sized claws.

Stoeckl was worried. And the problem of getting his money became further complicated by the heirs of one Benjamin Perkins of Worcester, Massachusetts, who for years had tried without success to collect a bill he claimed Russia owed him for ammunition and arms ordered during the Crimean War. Where Perkins once had offered to settle for $130,000, his heirs inflated their demands to $800,000, organized a stock company, and handed out interests in the claim to congressmen and others they believed to be in a position to force the State Department into making Russia settle. They attempted to block the Alaska appropriation measure in the hope that Stoeckl would pay them to go away. General Ben Butler of Massachusetts even introduced a resolution in the House to withhold $500,000 from the Alaska purchase money to satisfy the Perkins claim.

The efforts of the Perkins faction were fruitless. However, they tried again later, during Grant's administration, with Mrs. Grant's two brothers pushing the matter, and caused no end of trouble and embarrassment for Secretary of State Hamilton Fish. But they never did collect. In his biography of Fish, historian Allan Nevins points out that Perkins had no written contracts and says the whole thing probably was a fraud.

Meanwhile, Secretary Seward was stealing a march on the opposition by talking President Johnson into arranging the formal takeover of Russian-America. The climax came on October 18, 1867. As troop units representing the two nations stood at "present arms" on the tiny parade ground before the Russian governor's house at Sitka, the banner of Muscovy fluttered down and Old Glory was hauled to the top of the mast by the 15-year-old son of General Lovell H. Rousseau, the U.S. Commissioner for the transfer.

This latest move of Seward's did little to win over legislators who still resented the secrecy surrounding the original transaction. But by the time President Johnson's impeachment trial was over and the House got around to considering the appropriation bill, in the spring of 1868, tempers had cooled somewhat and much of the influential press now was pointing out the great potential advantages of our new possession. To some, national honor was at stake, too. It was unthinkable that we should ever haul down the Stars and Stripes, particularly when such an action would involve an insult to one of our "best friends"—Russia. The myth of Russian-American friendship still persisted.

The House began consideration of the Alaska appropriation bill on May 18. On July 14 it voted, by a comfortable margin, to pay Russia her $7,200,000 for nearly 600,000 square miles of territory—a bargain if there ever was one! The Senate quickly agreed, and President Andrew Johnson affixed his signature to the document on July 27, sixteen months after Seward and Stoeckl had signed the treaty.

But that was not the end of Stoeckl's troubles. Ugly stories of payoffs, circulating in Washington for months, brought on a congressional investigation. This revealed that the Russian minister's account in a District of Columbia bank had held $165,000, most of which ostensibly went for hiring lobbyists, influencing editors and, perhaps, for convincing lawmakers who lacked enthusiasm for handing over good taxpayers' dollars for what they considered a frozen wilderness.

Two lobbyists—Robert J. Walker, who had been Secretary of the Treasury in President Polk's cabinet, and Frederick P. Stanton, hired as "counsels" by Stoeckl—admitted to having received $26,000 from the Czar's minister. Small payments were traced to publicists who had been plumping for "Icebergia." But just who got the balance of the Russian slush fund remains a mystery to this day.

Andrew Johnson died in 1875. Many years afterward his private papers yielded a cryptic memorandum in his own handwriting detailing a conversation with Secretary

Seward in September 1868 which indicated the latter believed two prominent members of the House—Thaddeus Stevens of Pennsylvania and General Nathaniel Banks of Massachusetts—had been among the recipients of Stoeckl's largesse. By the time this came to light, the people involved had all passed on and nobody but the historians cared.

Although the Russian legation declined to offer testimony at the investigation, Stoeckl's name and reputation naturally came in for some rough handling. When it was all over, he requested his government to transfer him to another post. "Send me where I may breathe a purer air than that of Washington," he pleaded, forgetting that he himself, as well as the promoters of the Perkins claim, had contributed to the disagreeable odor on Capitol Hill. Instead of being transferred, he was pensioned off in 1868 at the age of 61 and, with his wife Eliza and their young son Alexander, departed for Paris, which remained his home until his death nearly a quarter of a century later.

Not many states can boast of a flag as strikingly beautiful as that flown by Alaska. The design—a field of deep blue with seven gold stars forming the big dipper and representing the gold mining history of the territory, and one more, slightly larger, representing the North Star and symbolizing the state's location in the far north—is unusual in its simplicity. Unusual, too, is the flag's history. It was created by a 13-year-old seventh-grader, Benny Benson, the son of an Aleut mother and a Swedish father.

He designed it as part of a contest for school children in Alaska sponsored by the American Legion in 1926 to give the future 49th state an official banner.

From 142 entries, Benny's was chosen as the most original and significant for the territory. His rewards were a gold watch bearing an enameled miniature of the new flag and a check for $1,000 to further his education. Benny passed away in Kodiak in 1972.

CENTURY-OLD SUPERMAN

An amazing phenomenon in the form of a "petrified man" was a feature in the news throughout the U.S. for many weeks during 1869. The excitement started on a farm in the small town of Cardiff, New York, when workers digging a well began to uncover the ten-foot figure of a man, eerily realistic, every detail suggestive of a once living human. Within a couple of days the owner of the land, William Newell, had erected a tent over the site and was charging 50¢ admission per person. Among those who rushed to see the "Cardiff Giant" was Andrew White, later the first president of Cornell University. In his autobiography he recalled the incident:

The roads were crowded with buggies, carriages, and even omnibuses from the city (Syracuse), and with lumber wagons from the farms—all laden with passengers. At the Newell farm we found a gathering which at first sight seemed like a county fair. In the midst was a tent, and a crowd was pressing for admission. Entering, we saw a large pit or grave and, at the bottom of it, perhaps five feet below the surface, an enormous figure, apparently of Onondaga gray limestone. It was a stone giant, with massive features, the whole body nude, with the limbs contracted as if in agony. Over its surface were minute punctures, like pores. Lying in its grave, with the subdued light from the roof of the tent falling upon it, and with the limbs contorted as if in a death struggle, it produced a weird effect. An air of great solemnity pervaded the place. Visitors hardly spoke above a whisper.

For many people, seeing this huge human form in the hushed stillness of a dimly-lit tent, still resting in the shallow grave where he had been discovered, the experience was almost a religious one. Most were spellbound by the sight. A newspaper reporter at the time remarked that he could not help feeling that he was in the presence of "a great and superior being."

Four physicians from the neighborhood examined the great discovery and declared it to be a petrified man. A prominent Syracuse doctor and antiquarian announced it was not a petrified man but a statue carved probably three centuries before by Jesuit priests who were known to have inhabited the area. The most respected scientists of the day were invited to come and give their opinions. Some came, and their pronouncements heated up the controversy. Meanwhile, with visitors crowding the roads, hotels and restaurants, business in the region around Cardiff flourished. Newell and a relative, George Hull, who appeared to be managing the show, were making a small fortune from the admission fees.

Showman P. T. Barnum came too and tried in vain to buy farmer Newell's find. A group of prominent Syracuse businessmen had better luck. For $30,000 they purchased a three-quarter interest in the petrified man. They moved him to Syracuse where, in addition to the crowds who continued to arrive in horse-drawn vehicles, the New York Central Railroad swelled the audience by arranging to stop its trains for ten minutes so the passengers could walk across the street and have a look at the giant. With some of the best known citizens of Syracuse backing the stone man, he became an object of civic interest and pride.

This beneficent excitement prevailed for six weeks after the exhuming of the giant. But slowly the disappointing truth became known. A Buffalo newspaper published the findings of Prof. Othniel Marsh of Yale, an eminent paleontologist and a man knowledgeable as well in the field of sculpture. He pronounced it a fraud, pointing out that it was made of gypsum and therefore of recent origin. Because the soil where the giant was found was damp, he explained, gypsum would have completely dissolved in a few years. This opinion came in the wake of much evidence belying the giant's authenticity. When the figure was removed from its pit to make the trip to Syracuse new scientific misgivings had arisen. The extensive erosion which had been so convincing at first turned out to be a dead giveaway—gypsum was found to be much more soluble in water than had been supposed. Also, local residents began to recall having seen a huge ironbound box being delivered to the Newell farm about a year earlier.

The hoax was the creation of Newell's relative, George Hull, who had hired two sculptors to carve the giant from a block of gypsum mined near Fort Dodge, Iowa. Hull had shipped the huge cargo to Newell's farm and the two men had buried it at night. The pores all over the body noted by Andrew White had been produced by whacking it with a wooden mallet set with darning needles. It had been "aged" with a sulphuric acid bath.

P. T. Barnum, not to be outdone by a couple of country boys, had a duplicate of the statue made and was soon advertising his creation as the original Cardiff Giant, implying that the one that Hull later took on tour was a fake.

After its popularity declined, the Cardiff Giant spent some forty years in storage. Later it had a number of owners, among them a Des Moines publisher who gave it a spot in the den of his home. The Farmers' Museum at Cooperstown, operated by the New York State Historical Association, acquired the Cardiff Giant in 1948 and continues to exhibit it among its collections.

STRANGERS IN PHARAOH-LAND

On June 5, 1975, Egypt reopened the Suez Canal, which had been closed since the 1967 Arab-Israeli War. The reopening was made possible partially through the efforts of the United States Navy, which retrieved more than 30,000 tons of ship wreckage from the canal. The Navy's help in clearing the debris of war from the Suez Canal was a reminder of another time, more than a century ago, when American expertise was highly regarded on the banks of the Nile. In those days Cairo's list of resident VIPs included a long string of names as thoroughly American as pumpkin pie. The man responsible for this influx of Americans was Egypt's ruler, or khedive, Ismail Pasha.

Any important traveler visiting Egypt's capital in the mid-1870's who asked to meet the khedive's military chief of staff would have been introduced to a uniformed dignitary with a white goatee and a handlebar mustache and wearing a bell-shaped headpiece called a fez but still seeming strangely out of place in the shadow of the Pyramids. The man seemed incongruous because he was Charles Pomeroy Stone, West Point graduate and in Civil War days a brigadier general of U.S. Volunteers.

Equally surprising would have been the close associates that General Stone might have presented. Among these were an ex-Confederate major general, William W. Loring, who, in 1847, had left an arm on a Mexican War battlefield, and an ex-Confederate brigadier general, Henry Hopkins Sibley, who served the khedive as a general of artillery. One could also have met a generous handful of other officers who less than a dozen years earlier had worn a uniform of Union blue or Confederate gray. All were now working together in the pay of Ismail Pasha, attempting to modernize Egypt's old-fashioned army and rebuild her crumbling coastal defenses.

Among the Americans gathered in Egypt's capital was an adventurer, Thaddeus Mott, a former colonel of cavalry in the Union army, who had been an advisor to Ismail Pasha during the elaborate ceremonies attendant on the original opening of the Suez Canal in 1869. Mott had lived in Constantinople (now Istanbul) where he was a favorite of the powerful Turkish sultan Abdul-Aziz, whose empire extended over much of northern Africa. Mott's father, a New York surgeon, had performed a successful operation upon the sultan thereby endearing his family to the ruler. As the sultan was Ismail's boss, Ismail was impressed with Mott's influence and was easily convinced by Mott of the need to modernize his army. Who better to train her soldiers, Mott asked, than Americans who recently had fought the biggest war to date? Mott soon hurried off across the Atlantic to recruit experts for the job, carrying the authority of the khedive of Egypt.

Mott sought the advice of William Tecumseh Sherman, now General of the Armies of the United States under President Ulysses S. Grant. Sherman made his recommendations, picking both old friends and respected old enemies. In the summer of 1870 the first contingent of Americans went to Cairo, to be followed over the next four years by others who brought the total to more than forty.

Some went because they needed employment; others, particularly the professional soldiers, because after years in uniform they had been unable to adjust to civilian life. Some went solely for adventure. A few were accompanied by wives and children.

The Americans attempted to superimpose a formal organization upon the armed forces but found that the centuries-old system of feudal-type, semi-autonomous units under independent pashas was so firmly entrenched that any change was difficult, if not impossible.

Soon after the Americans arrived, Ismail, Stone and Loring had several conferences to assess their position. Although the khedive was anxious to free Egypt from Turkish control and the Americans were eager for martial glory, they decided the immediate future needed a master plan to strengthen Egypt. Militarily, the seacoast defenses of the country would be improved and the army modernized and brought under central control. In a broader sense, Egypt's territory would be expanded by exploration and conquest. These new lands would help provide the resources to bolster Egypt's economy. Loring was put in charge of planning fortifications along the delta of the Nile and Stone would implement the reorganization of the army and the exploration and conquest necessary to expand the khedive's domain.

Loring met with limited success. He directed the building of the fortifications and the mounting of large caliber guns around the bay at Alexandria. But lack of finances halted the plans to construct additional hidden fortifications. His zeal was tempered not only by the lack of money from Ismail but also his troubles with the Muslim soldiers. They often chose the time appointed for troop inspection to take their morning devotions. As Muhammadans could pray whenever they chose with no interruptions once they began, the U.S. military men often faced gaping holes in the morning inspection lines. Upon checking the men's guns, the officers found them filthy, certainly not fit for inspection. Exasperated, the Americans complained to Egyptian officials who, in turn, accused the Americans of religious intolerance.

General Stone was assigned the positions of chief of staff and advisor to the khedive on military affairs. He faced the task of reorganizing the military forces, a job he never really accomplished. The existing army was organized into independent units whose ranks were filled by village sheiks who often resorted to force to fill their quotas.

The commanding pasha of each unit reported directly to the minister of war and to the khedive. These leaders did not want to submit to a central control as they were all-powerful within their realm. They performed all the tasks that Stone wanted to be taken over by his new general staff. Stone's initial plan was to build a staff in charge of inspection duties, supply, engineering, mapmaking and legal matters. In effect, the mapmaking and engineering departments eventually merged and were the only real functioning part of the staff.

The best work of this combined department was in directing exploration. Beginning in 1876, Stone sent out men to survey and map out future routes for roads and railroads and plan for irrigation works in the areas south of Cairo. The men cleaned out old abandoned waterholes, dug new wells and located reservoirs. They enlarged the country's boundaries, explored rivers and discovered lakes. Stone was instrumental in establishing schools for officers throughout the country and persuaded Ismail to promote only men who could read and write. In addition, a central school was set up in Cairo for noncommissioned officers.

In 1876 Ismail's army invaded neighboring Abyssinia and suffered a humiliating defeat. The soldiers were at a disadvantage before any firing began for they had been given modern rifles but no training in their use and many of them suffered from ophthalmia, a common affliction which made them partially blind. After the battle both American and Egyptian officers blamed each other. Fed up and disgusted, many Americans quit and went home.

Lack of money forced Ismail to terminate most of the remaining Americans by the summer of 1878. He awarded them six months severance pay together with travel money for returning to the United States.

Not only did most of the American service to Egypt come to an end but Ismail also lost his job. He began his rule with a genuine interest in modernizing his nation. He had remodeled an archaic customs service, established a postal system and brought in European contractors to build railways, telegraph lines, lighthouses and breakwaters.

Ismail's downfall had its roots in his conduct in office. Throughout his modernization program, he lived in the lavish style of an oriental potentate blessed with an endless supply of cash. In 1875 his extravagance necessitated selling his shares, the controlling interest, in the Suez Canal Company to Great Britain. This gave John Bull a toehold in Egypt that later was expanded to complete British domination which lasted until the end of World War I. Accordingly, in 1879 Ismail received his notice in a blunt telegram from the Turkish sultan addressed to the former khedive of Egypt.

"THE OLD CHISHOLM TRAIL"

A good rousing song can sometimes do more to preserve the memory of an important happening than a truckload of historic markers. Such seems to be the case with "The Old Chisholm Trail" (pronounced Chizzum), in all likelihood the oldest of all American cowboy songs. Through the medium of stanzas like those given on page 90, thousands of people who have never been near Texas, Oklahoma or Kansas have heard about the most famous of all the routes scoured out of the prairies a century ago by the flinty hoofs of millions of Texas longhorns. These rugged critters, urged along by equally rugged Texas cowhands, traveled overland from their breeding grounds in Texas to the Kansas railheads, where they were hurried on to market in cattle cars.

Named for an Indian trader, Jesse Chisholm, the historic route that has come to be a symbol of the great trail-driving era extended for a thousand miles. Its main stem originated near the mouth of the Rio Grande. It passed through Austin, Waco and Fort Worth, with many feeder

routes joining the main trail before it left Texas. From Fort
Worth the trail veered slightly to the west before crossing
the Red River and heading directly north through Oklahoma, then usually referred to as the Indian Nation. Entering Kansas at Caldwell, the trail touched Wichita and
ended at Abilene on the new Kansas Pacific Railroad.

There is no clue, not even in Southwest folklore, as to
who was the first to describe the rigors of the Chisholm
Trail in song. It probably was some musically inclined
Texan who had spent weeks, perhaps even months,
pushing longhorns north at the exasperatingly slow rate of
a dozen to fifteen miles a day—swimming rivers, outwit-
ting cow thieves, facing the dangers of sudden midnight
stampedes. On returning home he had regaled friends and
relatives with rough verses about his adventures.

As a stanza of "The Old Chisholm Trail" consists of only
two rhyming lines and a nonsensical chorus, it was the
simplest of songs to compose. Almost anyone could make
up such grass roots poetry, and it would appear that almost
every trail driver did. In addition to the handful of stanzas
on the following pages, there are hundreds more on record,
many of them too risqué to print. Personal experiences of
all kinds—humorous, lewd, tragic—were worked into the
song. Someone once said that if all the stanzas of "The Old
Chisholm Trail" were placed end to end, the song would be
longer than the trail. Melodies also are plentiful. Rarely
will the same tune be found in any two songbooks.

In his book *The Old-Time Cowhand*, Texas historian
Ramon F. Adams tells the story of an inebriated cowboy
who added to the song under rather unusual circumstances. His repetitious singing of "The Old Chisholm
Trail" had become so annoying that the bartender of the
saloon he was patronizing suggested he go elsewhere.

Finally this high-heeled Caruso was refused more drinks—the
bartender afterward said he wanted to get rid of that singin'
before it soured the whisky. But this cowboy was enjoyin' life,
and nothin' seemed to make 'im mad. The saloon was built high,
with a wooden porch 'bout five feet from the ground and with
wide steps that led to the street and hitch rack below. As he came

through the swingin' doors to make his way across the street to 'nother bar where his welcome hadn't been wore out, he was liftin' his feet like a sand hill crane walkin' up a riverbed. Halfway across the porch he let go with his acid tenor to continue the song he'd started inside:

"With my knees in the saddle an' my seat in the sky-y-y,
I'll quit punchin' cows in the sweet by an' by-y-y-y."

Jes' then he missed the steps and landed five feet below, the jar rattlin' his bones like throwin' down an armload of wood, but he kept standin' straight up. With hardly a break in his song, he continued in correct rhyme and rhythm:

"An, by God, they shore built them steps damned high-h-h-h."

The following is a more conventional rendering of the famous song.

THE OLD CHISHOLM TRAIL

Oh, come along, boys, and listen to my tale,
While I tell you all my troubles on the Old Chisholm Trail.

CHORUS
Come a ti yi yippy yippy yea, yippy yea,
Come a ti yi yippy yippy yea.

On a ten dollar horse and a forty dollar saddle,
I started in to punchin' Texas cattle.

It's bacon and beans most every day,
I'd rather be eatin' prairie hay.

It's cloudy in the west and a-lookin' like rain,
And my damned old slicker's in the wagon again.

No chaps, no slicker, and a-pourin' down rain;
I swear, by God, I'll never night-herd again.

My horse throwed me off just like I was a bird,
He throwed me off near the 2-U herd.

Last time I saw him he was goin' on the level,
A-kickin' up his heels and runnin' like the devil.

As soon as I recovered from that damned hard jolt
I got a job a-punchin' for Old Man Bolt.

Old Ben Bolt was a fine old man,
There always would be whiskey wherever he'd land.

On the herd one night when the leader broke the ranks,
I hit my horse on the shoulders and spurred him in the flanks.

The wind commenced to blow, and the rain commenced to fall,
An' it looked, by grab, like we was goin' to lose 'em all.

My feet in the stirrups and my rump in the saddle,
I hung and I rattled with those long-horned cattle.

We herded and we hollered, and we done very well,
Till the boss said, "Boys, let 'em go to Hell."

We all hit town, and we hit her on the fly,
And we bedded down the cattle on a hill close by.

Then we rounded 'em up, and we put 'em in the cars,
An' that was the end of the Bar-C-Bars.

I went to the boss to draw my roll;
He had me figured nine dollars in the hole.

I'll sell my outfit as fast as I can,
I won't punch cows for no damn man.

Goin' to sell my bridle, goin' to sell my saddle,
Goin' to monkey no more 'round the long-horn cattle.

GENERAL SHERIDAN
ENTERTAINS A GRAND DUKE

Early in January of 1872, youthful "Buffalo Bill" Cody, government scout and noted buffalo hunter, received an unusual order from Lieutenant General Philip Sheridan, commander of the Western Division of the United States Army. It instructed Cody to find the famous Sioux Chief Spotted Tail and request him to move his village to a site on Red Willow Creek, some fifty miles south of the Union Pacific Railroad station at North Platte, Nebraska. Buffalo Bill was then to await Sheridan's arrival at North Platte.

Another who was ordered by Sheridan to report to him at North Platte was George Armstrong Custer, who, during the Civil War days, had done the impossible by climbing to the rank of brigadier general at the age of twenty-three. Now thirty-two, Custer was serving at a sleepy army post in Kentucky, following five years of service on the Western plains, fighting Indians and, in quiet periods, hunting buffalo. With some anticipation after receiving Sheridan's telegram, Custer packed his best suit of fringed buckskin and his sealskin cap and caught a west-bound train.

What was General Sheridan up to?

Taking advantage of a lull in Indian warfare on the frontier, the commander of the army's Western Division was arranging a buffalo hunt—history's most spectacular buffalo hunt—to honor a member of the Russian royal family.

The guest who was to be entertained by renowned Buffalo Bill and dashing young cavalryman Custer and who would get a close look at Indian life in the village of Chief Spotted Tail, was Grand Duke Alexis, fourth son of Czar Alexander II. A handsome lad of 21, Alexis was tall, strongly built, with bushy sideburns and blue eyes. He had a dignified bearing, spoke English well and his personal charm, especially among the ladies, was said to be overwhelming.

93

The Duke and a small party of Russian dignitaries were touring the United States. Although to many Americans he represented an absolute monarchy, actually, there was a tentative sympathy between the two lands. America had given moral support to Russia during the Crimean War and it was reciprocated during the American Civil War. Serfdom and slavery had been abolished at approximately the same time. So Czar Alexander had sent Alexis on a state visit in order to cement a palpable friendship between the two countries. The United States reacted graciously, and hospitality was the key word in the lavish cordiality accorded the Grand Duke.

General Sheridan's assignment was to introduce the royal visitor to the American West and the most unusual outdoor "sport" then offered by North America—buffalo shooting, an exciting pastime that completely disappeared a few years later as the great shaggy beasts, once counted in the millions, were almost wiped out. But in 1872 the buffalo were still plentiful, and hopes for a successful hunt were high early on the morning of January 13 when the Grand Duke's special train, with Sheridan aboard, pulled into North Platte. Headquarters for the hunt would be luxurious "Camp Alexis," named in honor of the Imperial guest, and set up on Sheridan's orders fifty miles to the south of the railroad in a cottonwood grove on Red Willow Creek, with friendly Chief Spotted Tail's village close by. Reliable reports said that buffalo herds were numerous in the vicinity.

Following breakfast in the railroad dining car, members of the hunting party prepared for the eight-hour journey to Camp Alexis. Their guide over the roadless prairie was Buffalo Bill Cody, Sheridan's favorite prairie scout. He was about thirty years old, over six feet tall, fine-looking and well-spoken. He was mounted on a fine horse, "Buckskin Joe," who was known to have carried him eighty miles one day in escaping Indians. He wore the buckskin suit and long hair that later became his trademarks, which caused people to remark that if his flowing hair had been festooned with feathers, he would have been mistaken for a great Indian chief.

The Duke and General Sheridan followed Cody in an open wagon drawn by four horses. Sheridan's officers and the other Russians rode in army ambulances pulled by mules. They left North Platte and hit the rugged prairie on a run, causing a newspaper reporter who went along to write later that he and everyone else could now appreciate what travel was like in the days of the overland stagecoaches before the "iron horse" on glistening rails spanned the continent. A few miles from North Platte the travelers were met by a military escort, one of two troops of the Second Cavalry stationed at Camp Alexis during the hunt.

A reporter with the party enthusiastically maintained that the "Duke seemed to be carried away with the grandeur of the country and the excitement of the trip, and the Russians were highly entertained by the yarns of their military escort about their perilous adventures on the frontier in the past."

An account of the remainder of the trip is described in *The Grand Duke Alexis in the United States of America* compiled by William Warren Tucker.

A halt was made at the Medicine River, where horses were changed and a light lunch was speedily dispatched. However, when we resumed our run the speed with which we were proceeding produced some broken springs and spokeless wheels. Just before the sun had sunk below the distant hills, and as we ascended some rising ground, we came in full view of a splendid military camp. The Stars and Stripes were seen flying from a towering flagstaff on a broad plateau on the bank of Red Willow Creek. A cheer arose from every member of our party as this scene burst upon our sight. A few moments more and the Second United States Cavalry band was playing the Russian hymn.

Not only were the Russians regaled with full military honors, they were also treated to the colorful arrival of Spotted Tail and one hundred of his warriors and chiefs. And it had not been easy to set up. When Buffalo Bill had been sent to find Spotted Tail and present him with Sheridan's proposition, he had to negotiate a secret meeting with the chief, for his scalp was worth much to many young bucks whom he had formerly encountered. Spotted Tail had agreed to stage, for the General and his guests, a buffalo hunt, exhibitions of horsemanship, sham fights and a grand war dance. Cody could only hope that sham would not become reality.

The accommodations for the camp guests are here described. There were guest tents, of course, in addition to the rows of tents set up for the cavalrymen and other soldiers doing the work at Camp Alexis.

Twelve new wall tents, fitted up with all camp conveniences (and the Duke's was carpeted), are arranged in a line for the guests. The dining room of our camp is formed of two large tents and is very handsomely festooned inside with flags. A sumptuous banquet was presented for the guests. The meal included different varieties of game found on the Western prairies. Choice wines were served with the different courses. After dinner songs were sung and yarns spun over the blazing campfire, and one by one the members of the party retired to their tents to sleep, perhaps to dream of the expected buffalo hunt on the morrow.

In the morning, the weather for the hunt was perfect, more like September than January. In this, General Sheridan was just plain lucky. A week later western Nebraska was hit by a howling blizzard. Buffalo were reported about 15 miles from camp. The hunters were soon on the scene. The Duke was dressed simply for the occasion, buttons bearing the Romanoff coat of arms were all that decorated his gray jacket, whereas others in his party could not forego their gold, lace and other royal trappings. Cody and Custer, sporting their buckskins, had coached Alexis in the use of American firearms, and found he was a capital shot, having hunted big game in Asia. Cody allowed Alexis to ride Buckskin Joe, who, as well as being a long-distance runner, was an excellent buffalo horse who would keep pace with a buffalo until it was shot and immediately gallop up to the next.

The Duke, having been accorded the first shot of the day, downed a big bull. The pace was set, but time was called for champagne all around. Alexis' aides certainly came prepared with the necessities (it must be remembered that luxuries were forsworn for this trip). Then the hunt resumed and the party bagged between twenty and thirty animals. The Grand Duke chose to take back to Russia as trophies the head and horns of a handsome cow he had killed. Buffalo steaks were enjoyed that night at both Camp Alexis and Spotted Tail's village.

The next day the hunt continued; Alexis and everyone else bagged more buffalo. With the helter-skelter galloping over the prairie it was a wonder no humans were shot. An old Cody tale goes that a highlight of the day was the dexterous feat of a husky Indian named Two Lance, who reportedly drove an arrow clear through a running buffalo. Two Lance asked Custer to give the wondrous weapon to the Grand Duke, and Alexis reciprocated the honor by ceremoniously presenting the warriors with money, blankets and hunting knives that evening.

The program for that evening at Camp Alexis included a great Indian war dance to illustrate the "curious customs of the red men. It consist(ed) chiefly in each warrior arising and recounting the history of his exploits, at the same time dancing in the circle formed by his hearers, and keeping time to the monotonous music of the musicians, who beat away on a kind of drum, while he extol(ed) himself in his native language."

The spectacle was so realistic it sent shivers down the spines of the white onlookers, but there did appear a diversion in the lovely presence of Spotted Tail's daughter. The "dusky maiden" became "the object of marked attention on the part of some of the gallant young warriors from circles of (the white man's) higher form of civilization." Her rosy cheeks would have been the envy of all the ladies at a Presidential ball. Custer himself paid tribute to Miss Spotted Tail with jewels.

When the festivities were concluded and the Indians returned to their village for the night, Chief Spotted Tail and his wife and daughter stayed behind and the chief asked to speak with General Sheridan on matters concerning his people. Sheridan invited the three Indians into his tent along with Alexis and a few of the latter's aides. A reporter described the scene and it is recounted in *The Grand Duke Alexis in the United States of America.*

The Duke reclined on Sheridan's bed, Custer sat on the table, Spotted Tail, with his wife and daughter, sat on Sheridan's baggage, and others occupied the remaining limited space within the tent. In accordance with Indian usage, Spotted Tail first took a smoke. When he had finished, he handed the pipe to his wife, and then, in a dignified and deliberate manner, arose, and through the interpreter, addressed some sensible remarks to General Sheridan.

After expressing his pleasure at being invited to participate in the buffalo hunt for Duke Alexis, the old chief asked that his people be allowed to hunt outside their reservation until their farms could be cultivated to produce enough food for the tribe to be self-sustaining. He also complained about the way the reservation trading post was run. He said that when he had been in Washington he had seen that "the white man was not compelled to trade at a single store or with one trader, but could go to any store; and if one trader asked what seemed to be too high a price he could go and bargain with another; but such was not the case with Spotted Tail and his people." The Great Father had only allowed them one trader on their reservation. This he did not think was right; and in order to have some safety against extortion he requested that at least one more trader might be permitted on the reservation. Through an interpreter, Sheridan granted the first request as long as Spotted Tail maintained peace, and promised he would have a talk with the Great Father in Washington about the other matter.

Next morning, after their two hard days in the saddle, the Imperial hunting party returned to North Platte. Duke Alexis, after expressing his thanks and making gifts to his hosts, again boarded his special train, in the company of Sheridan and Custer, to continue his wining and dining across the country.

HOME SWEET SODDY

Imagine yourself standing in the middle of a prairie and not being able to see a single tree in any direction. Eighty or ninety years ago that was the view for many a homesteader on his 160 acres of free government land, particularly in Kansas, Nebraska, Oklahoma, or the Dakotas.

Because trees were scarce, there was little or no wood for building houses. No stone was available, nor was there clay for making bricks. So there was nothing to do but build homes, schoolhouses, churches, blacksmith shops, stores, and newspaper offices out of the thick prairie sod provided by the tough, matted roots of waist-high buffalo grass or bluestem that covered the landscape as far as the eye could see. Crude sod dugouts like the one shown above also were a common sight in the early days.

The first step in house-building was to mow a large patch of prairie. Then strips of turf four or five inches thick and about a foot wide were turned over with a special sod-cutting plow pulled by oxen or horses. These long strips were chopped with a sharp spade or an ax into lengths a man could handle. At the construction site, a layer of these sod blocks was placed on the ground, grass side down, to form the base of the wall, a wall customarily thirty inches thick, all the way around the building. The first layer was leveled carefully before a second was placed on top, again grass side down, and staggered to cover up cracks where mice and snakes might hide. Making everything fit snugly was an exacting and vital part of sod house construction; these prairie "brick-layers" had no mortar to fill the cracks and hold things together.

Window and door frames were nailed together from packing boxes or whatever lumber could be bought in the nearest town or sawed from a few trees perhaps available along the creek beds. More layers of sod were added until the walls reached their desired height. Virtually all soddies were only one story high.

Glass windows were purchased when there was enough money; otherwise, the homesteader made do with heavy oiled paper, even burlap sacking, until times got better. The door was made of planks nailed together. As hardware usually was as scarce as wood, door hinges often were pieces of old leather belting. Inside walls were plastered or whitewashed. The floor might have to remain dirt until the first few corns crops were sold and boards could be bought.

The roof invariably was the biggest problem. Many were built of thin wooden planking nailed to rafters and covered by a layer of sod, this time with the grass side up. Such a covering turned green with the spring rains—even had wildflowers sprouting from it—and, from numerous accounts, often leaked like a sieve. The sod on the roof served as insulation and sometimes kept it from being ripped off in a strong wind.

Another fairly common type of roof, one made of brush and finished off with a layer of clay, is described in a slim volume, *Sod House Memories Volume II,* published in 1967 by the Sod House Society of Nebraska. E. E. Bowers tells about roofing the soddy built in 1870 by his parents in York County, some fifty miles west of Lincoln, Nebraska.

There was very little timber along Lincoln Creek. They (his father and neighbors) had to go to the Platte River (about 15 miles) to get poles for the ridge poles and rafters for the roof. In making the roof, on top of the rafters they laid small willow brush, and on top of that a layer of coarse slough grass, and on top of that they miss-matched two layers of sod. In finishing the roof, they put on two or three inches of clay. On the underside of the rafters they tacked building paper to keep the dust and chaff from sifting down into everything. This made a good roof for ordinary weather but when we had a two or three day rain, the water soaked through this roof and it began to leak.

Then we had to put oilcloth over the beds to keep them dry, and mother would have to stand on a chair with a dishpan and a sharp stick to make holes in the building paper, to let the water out so the paper would not burst.

And there were natural disasters. Along with terrible fires and tornadoes, the prairie homesteader feared the sudden deadly hailstorms. In Roger L. Welsch's book *Sod Walls*, Leota Runyan of Mason City, Nebraska recalls a storm that made a lasting impression on her:

One evening when my oldest brother was old enough to go after cows, a cloud came up quickly. Mother, who was worried about my oldest brother, watched it anxiously. Soon he came over the hill in sight. Big drops of rain started to fall; then an occasional large hailstone fell. My brother began to pick up the hailstones, not thinking of what was behind him. When the hail became very thick and large, mother saw my brother fall. She quickly grabbed the fuel basket, dumped the contents on the floor and dashed out of the door with the basket over her head. She got to my brother and the two got under the basket for protection.

My father was in the field with four horses hitched to a disc. He unhitched the horses and raced toward the barn. He reached the granary first and stopped in its shelter. One horse was close enough to the granary to be partially protected. That helped him hold on to the others while they reared against the pounding hail, but Dad held on to the reins with one hand out in the storm through it all.

In the meantime, my little brothers and I were in the house but the windows on that side of the house crashed in and glass flew all over the house. My little brothers screamed and I ran to get pillows to hold to the window. This calmed the boys.

When the storm was over, my oldest brother came in with a bump on his head the size of a goose egg. One of my dad's hands swelled to twice its normal size and my mother had a cut on her forehead that was bleeding so badly that her face was covered with streams of blood. At the sight of this my brothers and I set up a terrible scream again.

I was always afraid of hail after that. When a cloud came up, I would always ask Mother if it was going to hail. How comforting it was, when in her judgement, she would say, "No, there is no hail in that cloud." Or sometimes she would say, "Oh, this is August. It seldom hails in August."

Nineteenth-century sodbusters had a sheaf of home-made songs to illuminate their own particular page in the book of American pioneer history. One of the best is "The Little Old Sod Shanty on the Claim," written in the early 1880's by some lonely bachelor homesteader who had bet Uncle Sam five years of his life against 160 acres of free land.

The stanzas that follow were printed on the reverse side of a sod house photograph taken in 1885 by Jasper N. Templeman of Miller, South Dakota, and sold to railway travelers by another picturesque character of bygone days, the "train butcher."

No one really knows who composed this down-to-earth word portrait of a solitary man living on the treeless plains miles from civilization, his clothes covered with dough as he tries to cook on a stove fueled by twisted hanks of prairie hay. Photographer Templeman's text does say, however, that the words were written to be sung to the tune of an older song whose subject was a "little old log cabin in the lane."

I am looking rather seedy now while holding down my claim,
And my victuals are not always served the best,
And the mice play slyly 'round me as I lay me down to sleep

In my little old sod shanty on the claim.
Yet I rather like the novelty of living in this way,
Though my bill of fare is always rather tame,
And I'm happy as a clam, on this land of Uncle Sam,
In my little old sod shanty on the claim.

CHORUS

The hinges are of leather and the windows have no glass,
While the roof, it lets the howling blizzard in,
And I hear the hungry coyote, as he sneaks up through the grass
'Round my little old sod shanty on the claim.

But when I left my Eastern home, so happy and so gay,
To try to win my way to wealth and fame,
I little thought I'd come down to burning twisted hay
In my little old sod shanty on the claim.
My clothes are plastered o'er with dough, and I'm looking like a
    fright,
And everything is scattered 'round the room
And I fear if P. T. Barnum's man should get his eyes on me
He would take me from my little cabin home.

I wish that some kind hearted Miss would pity on me take
And extricate me from the mess I'm in.
The angel—how I'd bless ner if this her home she'd make
In my little old sod shanty on the claim.
And when we'd made our fortunes on these prairies of the West,
Just as happy as two bedbugs we'd remain,
And we'd forget our trials and our troubles as we rest
In our little old sod shanty on the plain.

And if heaven should smile upon us with now and then an heir
To cheer our hearts with honest pride to flame,
O, then we'd be content for the years that we have spent
In our little old sod shanty on the claim.
When time enough had 'lapsed and all those little brats
To man and honest womanhood have grown,
It won't be half so lonely when around us we shall look
And see other old sod shanties on the claim!

103

ELISHA GRAY, TELEPHONE PIONEER

A difference of only a few hours in filing documents with the U.S. Patent Office in Washington, D.C., made all the difference in the world in the lives of two men. Because of the way our patent system works, Alexander Graham Bell got all the credit for inventing the telephone and his rivals, among them able inventor Elisha Gray, became "footnotes" in telephone history.

In 1871, when 24-year-old Scottish-born Bell arrived in Boston to begin teaching the deaf, Elisha Gray's name was well-known in the electrical field. Twelve years Bell's senior, Gray was responsible for numerous improvements in the telegraph. He also had invented the electric annunciator, a device once widely used to summon servants in hotels and large private homes. He was a founding partner in Gray & Barton, a company which later became Western Electric, the manufacturing arm of American Telephone & Telegraph. Before attempting to send the human voice over a wire, Gray, as did Bell, labored hard and long over the "harmonic telegraph," an instrument designed to use the notes of the musical scale to accomplish multi-transmission of messages over a telegraph line.

On St. Valentine's Day in 1876, Gray visited the Patent Office and filed a "caveat," a confidential report stating that he was well along with the development of an instrument for transmitting human speech electrically. By the strangest of coincidences, earlier on the same day an attorney for Bell had filed for a patent on the telephone, even though Bell had not yet succeeded in sending speech over a wire. Since a caveat entitled Gray to be alerted should anyone else later file papers relating to the same invention, had the order of filing been reversed he probably would have had a fair shot at what turned out to be the handsomest of prizes—the telephone patent.

In 1876 the Patent Office moved fast. On March 7, just three weeks after filing an application and actually three days before he and his assistant Thomas Watson first transmitted the human voice over an electrical circuit, Bell was granted U.S. Patent No. 174,465, the most valuable ever issued in America.

A few months later Bell demonstrated his instrument at the Centennial Exposition in Philadelphia. In less than a year the first commercial telephone was in operation. The going, however, was rough for the new enterprise. In 1877, Bell's financial backers offered to sell the telephone to Western Union, then the giant of the communications field. President William Orton of Western Union turned it down. Two years later, when the public began showing a preference for the new way of communicating, Orton enlisted the inventive genius of Gray and Thomas Edison and entered the telephone business. The Bell organization went to court claiming infringement, and won.

In the aftermath of the lawsuit, Gray formally conceded that Bell was the inventor of the telephone. But seven years later he had second thoughts and went into court himself claiming fraud on Bell's part and skulduggery in the Patent Office. Gray contended that an unscrupulous patent examiner had let Bell's attorney see his papers. But his efforts were in vain. The courts backed the Patent Office, as they did in hundreds of other actions brought against the Bell interests.

In spite of his heartbreaking disappointments, Gray continued with electrical research. During his lifetime he acquired 70 patents. His best known invention, after the annunciator, was the telautograph, a device still used for transmitting facsimile writing and drawings instantaneously. For 20 years prior to his death, in 1901, Gray served as a professor of dynamic electricity at Oberlin College in his native Ohio.

MYSTERY MOTOR

A combination of compressed air and hot air provided purported inventor John Keely with a good living for nearly thirty years. It even got him commemorated in *Who Was Who in America*. The line attributed to the great showman P.T. Barnum—"There's a sucker born every minute"—was firmly believed by Keely.

Who was this man who could hoodwink people into believing he had, in fact, discovered a new source of power which he claimed would one day propel an ocean liner across the Atlantic on the energy concealed in a gallon of tap water? John Worrell Keely was orphaned in infancy and received no formal education after the age of twelve. He is known to have been a carpenter, an orchestra leader and a circus performer before turning his attention to scientific "discovery."

Perhaps his success in this area, though bogus, was neither too strange nor inexplicable. He lived in an era of great inventions. The telephone and the electric light had become realities; fortunes were being made in steel, oil and electric railways. Now Keely, a physically impressive man with a remarkable gift of gab, came to public notice in the early 1870's claiming to have discovered a new physical force resulting from the intermolecular vibrations of ether. His slickly disarming presentation of this somewhat unintelligible claim was bought by an impressionable public. The fact that the source of this force was water, which is readily and plentifully available, made the discovery that much more commercially titillating. He astounded people with demonstrations of his mysterious machines that appeared to run on water and were cranked up by vibrations from tuning forks and harmonicas. He obviously derived his vocabulary from his musical background and he combined it with a disguising expertise garnered from his circus connections.

The news media and many in the scientific community reacted with a natural skepticism to this man and his claims, but investors flocked to enlist under the Keely banner, hoping to be in on the ground floor when the next significant scientific advance was announced. Keely's inability to as yet apply his newly unearthed source of power to existing machinery was merely an annoying detail. Someday soon he would succeed, his followers insisted, and then there would be a new crop of millionaires. Their incentive to believe was of course predicated on the promise of financial gain. Organizing an amply financed Keely Motor Company was easily accomplished.

When time passed and there were no results in the way of products or dividends, Keely quieted his investors' fears by breathlessly announcing some new and startling development with a long name. He never applied for a patent. To do so, he argued, would be to give away his secret. In 1880, however, the stockholders had lost patience; Keely had not perfected his motor, so the company ceased making payments to him and brought suit to compel the disclosure of his secret. He would have faced bankruptcy had not a *deus ex machina* appeared in the form of Mrs. Clara Bloomfield-Moore.

Mrs. Moore was a widowed heiress from Philadelphia.

She had inherited five million dollars from her husband, a paper manufacturer. A picturesque figure, Mrs. Moore was known on two continents as a collector of fine art and had all the right social and cultural connections. She entertained the greatest literary personages of her time, including Robert and Elizabeth Barrett Browning. A writer of sentimental novels herself, she was most concerned with the social instability of America. So she codified social laws into *Sensible Etiquette of the Best Society,* issued under the pen name Mrs. H. O. Ward, and it became the most widely read tract for the newly rich who wanted to behave correctly in every situation.

Now Mrs. Moore was obviously of a strong-willed disposition and therefore very much in charge of her own life. She was considered to have a remarkable amount of scientific knowledge "for a woman," and like a noted Philadelphian of another era, Benjamin Franklin, she corresponded with scientists all over the world. It was inevitable that she would hear of the "inventor," John Keely, and his plight. She met him, liked him and gave him her moral and financial support for the next fifteen years. This allowed him to keep alive the fiction that he was on the threshold of a discovery that would change the world.

Mrs. Moore was only representative of the kind of blind belief evidenced by so many. In September of 1884 the Keely Motor Company stockholders persuaded Keely to demonstrate publicly at Sandy Hook, New Jersey, his mysterious force, supposedly harnessed in a "vaporic" gun. As he alighted from the train placed at his disposal by the Philadelphia and Reading Railroad, the band played "Some Day." The crowd was almost reverential. The following conversation was recounted by *The New York Times:*

"He's come and he's got it with him," said Mr. Peabody in a subdued voice to a group of gentlemen.

"It? What?" asked a dozen voices.

"I don't know," said Mr. Peabody in perplexed tones. "Nobody knows. It. The force. Etherealized vaporic power."

"Oh, yes! Yes! Of course," said the gentlemen, as though they understood thoroughly, and felt convinced that if they went into a drugstore and asked for 10 cents worth of etherealized vaporic power it would be given to them in a small bottle . . . .

"How does Mr. Keely get the first start? Ah ha! As he said to me, 'No one but scientific men can understand it, but I assure you it's beautiful.' "

"But what is this vapor?"

"No one but Keely knows . . . ."

Keely had brought with him a small cannon and a container of his mysterious "force" brewed in his Philadelphia laboratory. Without generating either heat or smoke, Keely fired a number of shots into a target 500 feet away, then drove projectiles through heavy spruce planks at close range. And he received reams of publicity.

However, a sour note came from *The Times* a few days later:

The "etherealized vaporic force" which was so liberally poured into the ears of a large and gullible public by Mr. John Keely of Philadelphia . . . does not seem to have intoxicated Lieutenant E. L. Zalinski, who is wedded to science for its own sake and is in no way connected with companies of any description. The Lieutenant witnessed the experiments at Sandy Hook and then told President A. R. Edey (of the Keely Motor Company) that with the same plant he could perform exactly the same experiments . . . with compressed air.

Subsequent events proved Lieutenant Zalinski to be a keen observer. A month later, Keely invited reporters to his laboratory to see his motor, an apparatus six feet long, in action. The experiments were apparently less impressive than the oysters and champagne which were served, and Keely's explanations were "unintelligible jargon." *The Times* reporter commented:

"Mr. Keely, newspapermen are naturally suspicious, and you must pardon me for asking you what I do. But you have requested our presence here and have desired us to make what inquiries we choose. Now, we see a great deal of power is here, and we cannot understand how it is produced. And we think that there may be something in the room below which produces this power. Can't you let us look into the room below, which is locked up?"

Mr. Keely was greatly taken aback at this. He waited for an instant before replying and then said he would certainly not show what was in the room downstairs. What was there, he said, was an apparatus which he was constructing for a California party designed for the lifting of heavy weights and therefore he could not show it.

Skepticism reared its head again three years later when a machinist for the Keely Company announced he was going to write an exposé for the "edification of Wall Street and this too confiding world." He said that the outside shape of Keely's motor had little to do with its working parts and furthermore it used not one drop of water: "The water story is bosh."

Still, the stockholders, the interested public and Mrs. Moore persisted in their trust for years, always held by Keely's claims of incipient breakthroughs. Keely died in 1898 and the news precipitated Mrs. Moore's decline and death a few months later.

Shortly thereafter, a group of prominent engineers and college professors brought together by a Philadelphia newspaper and Mrs. Moore's son spent more than a week taking Keely's laboratory apart, searching for his alleged secret. With the appearance of this group's findings in the press on January 19, 1899, Keely investors began kicking themselves. Lieutenant Zalinski, *The Times* reporter and the machinist could all have said, "We told you so." The gist of the report was that it was not the energy in water that made the famed Keely motor turn over. It was compressed air from a reservoir cleverly concealed in the basement of his laboratory. Conducting as the orchestra leader he once was, Keely had struck a chord with Barnum's "suckers," and the result was a chorus of false belief.

A HAND FOR GENERAL GRANT

One day in May of 1884, General Ulysses S. Grant made the startling discovery that he was flat broke. This was shocking indeed for the man who had led the armies of the North to victory in the Civil War, had twice been elected President of the United States, and was considered a well-to-do gentleman.

Grant's stay in the White House (1869-1877) had been badly marred by the scandalous conduct of men he had appointed to public office. Nevertheless, after a four-year breather during which he had toured the world and had had honors heaped on him at every turn, he had made a strong bid for the Republican presidential nomination again in 1880. Failing in this, the aging former soldier retired from public life and entered the business world, where he was as much out of his element as he had been when in politics.

Moving to New York from Washington, Grant put his capital into a new Wall Street investment banking firm,

Grant & Ward, one of whose partners was his son. The other partner was a smooth-talking young man whom Grant believed to be a financial wizard. After three years the wizardry resulted in the disappearance of Grant's money, along with that of many friends and relatives who had believed the general's magic name would make them all rich. The swindle, which put Ferdinand Ward behind bars, left the 62-year-old former president not only penniless, but heavily in debt.

Prior to this disaster, Grant had been approached by *Century*, a popular monthly magazine, about writing a series of articles on his Civil War campaigns. Unsure of his writing ability, the great military leader had declined. Now, having to depend on the generosity of friends even for the money to pay his household bills, he said yes to another offer from *Century* and set about producing three articles.

Among the general's many friends was Samuel Clemens, who lived in Hartford, Connecticut, and had written many well-received books under the pseudonym Mark Twain. While on a visit to New York, Clemens learned through a chance encounter with Richard Watson Gilder, editor of *Century*, that the nation's most prominent private citizen was to receive only $500 each for these contributions that were expected to bring the magazine hundreds of new subscribers.

In his autobiography the creator of Tom Sawyer and Huckleberry Finn branded this proposal "not only the monumental injustice of the 19th century but of all centuries." Then he added: "Gilder went on to say that it had been impossible, months before, to get General Grant to write a single line, but now that he once got started, it was going to be impossible to stop him again; that, in fact, General Grant had set out deliberately to write his memoirs in full, and to publish them in book form."

On receiving this astonishing news about Grant's memoirs, Clemens went into action. The very next morning he was knocking on the general's door. Grant confirmed what Gilder had said about the relatively small fee for the magazine articles. As for the proposed war memoirs, a contract had been drawn up, but fortunately, had not been signed. When Clemens took a look at the contract, he saw red. He described his reaction in *Mark Twain's Autobiography:*

Now here was a book that was morally bound to sell several hundred thousand copies the first year of its publication, and yet the *Century* people had had the hardihood to offer General Grant the very same 10-per-cent royalty that they would have offered to any unknown Comanche Indian whose book they had reason to believe might sell 3,000 or 4,000 or 5,000 copies.

If I had not been acquainted with the *Century* people, I would have said that this was a deliberate attempt to take advantage of a man's ignorance and trusting nature to rob him; but I do know the *Century* people, and therefore I know that they had no such base intentions as these, but were simply making their offer out of their boundless resources of ignorance. They were anxious to do book publishing as well as magazine publishing, and had tried one book already, but owing to their inexperience, had made a failure of it.

Samuel Clemens could speak with authority. In addition to being a widely read author, he recently had become a highly successful publisher of his own works. He strongly urged Grant not to sign the contract with *Century* but to talk with other publishers about his proposed memoirs and take the best offer. Clemens also put in his own bid on publishing the book, firmly believing that there would be a terrific demand for it from Union veterans and others keenly concerned with what Grant had to say about his military campaigns. Although the Civil War had been over for nearly twenty years, interest in its battles still ran high. The general himself doubted that 25,000 copies of his work would be sold, which bears out one of the sage remarks credited to Clemens—"It is difference of opinion that makes horse races." The result was that Clemens got the book for his own publishing house, Charles L. Webster & Co. of New York. Webster, a Clemens nephew by marriage, was the salaried manager with a small financial interest.

With the contract signed, a $10,000 advance royalty was quickly arranged for the general. Freed, at least temporarily, from money worries, the old soldier, now suffering from throat cancer, got to work and turned out two volumes that rank among the world's great military narratives. He completed his writing task only a few days before his death in July 23, 1885.

The book was sold by subscription. Even before the presses started rolling, orders for 100,000 sets had been received. On February 27, 1886, Clemens had the pleasure of mailing to Mrs. Grant a royalty check for $200,000. Subsequent royalties brought the total for the general's heirs close to half a million dollars.

It was no surprise to Clemens when he, too, made a small fortune on Grant's *Personal Memoirs*. But when he tried the same thing with the war recollections of two other famous Union generals—Philip H. Sheridan and George B. McClellan—the results were only so-so. These near failures were followed by *The Life of Pope Leo XIII* in six languages, which became a drug on the market, and a many-volumed *Library of American Literature*, a costly mistake that necessitated heavy borrowing to keep it going. Then a mechanical typesetter that Clemens had backed heavily refused to work properly and he lost out to Ottmar Mergenthaler's Linotype machine. In 1894, at the age of fifty-nine, Samuel Clemens was bankrupt—in the same fix his friend Ulysses Grant had been in ten years earlier.

But the famous author and humorist made his comeback, too. He embarked on a worldwide lecture tour and wrote more books. In less than four years he had paid off all his debts. When he passed away, in 1910, he left an estate valued at more than half a million dollars.

BRODIE DID IT
THE HARD WAY

New words and phrases become part of the American language every day. Most come from very interesting and often unexpected sources. Take the word "brodie," for example. In a three-inch-thick unabridged dictionary it is defined as "a suicidal leap, especially from a bridge."

The word was coined when an unemployed former New York newsboy named Steve Brodie, 23 years old and the father of three children, jumped 120 feet from the then three-year-old Brooklyn Bridge into the East River on July 23, 1886. To others on the bridge at the time it certainly looked like a suicidal leap. But Brodie had something far different in mind. He hit the river feet first, quickly bobbed to the surface and was pulled into a rowboat manned by friends who were cooperating in the dangerous publicity stunt.

The next morning Steve Brodie was on the front pages of the newspapers. *The New York Times* devoted nearly two columns on page 1 to his exploit and his subsequent detention by the police, who charged him not only with attempted suicide but with intoxication, the latter the result of all the spirits poured into the shivering high diver by well-wishers at the station house.

After a night in the well-known prison, the Tombs, a sobered Brodie was taken before a judge who had difficulty finding an applicable ruling. No one had ever jumped from the Brooklyn Bridge and lived to tell about it. So the case was continued until a later date and Steve was released on bail supplied by his alderman. Accompanied by an admiring crowd of men and boys, he walked cockily down the street into the arms of an enterprising lawyer who offered him $100 a week to exhibit himself in a Coney Island museum and tell of his adventure.

Brodie spoiled this by insisting the engagement be for ten weeks. However, he was signed up by Alexander's Museum in the Bowery, where he elaborated daily on his daring leap for the benefit of wide-eyed hayseeds. He appeared in several other museums and then opened a tavern at 114 Bowery that for years attracted well-known figures in the boxing world and became a mecca for slumming parties.

Somebody started a rumor that Brodie's great leap had been a fake, that a dummy had been dropped from the bridge while Steve himself hid near a dock and swam out to be rescued at the proper moment. To counter this base canard, Brodie decided to go over Niagara Falls in a rubber suit. As a warm-up for Niagara he leaped 90 feet into the basin below the Falls of the Passaic River at Paterson, N.J., wearing only red flannel underwear, and then leaped 60 feet at Pawtucket Falls, R.I.

A month later, Brodie tackled Niagara Falls. To avoid being stopped by the police, he donned his rubber suit at 5:30 in the morning and paddled out to the middle of the river above Horseshoe Falls on the Canadian side. Over he went in a cloud of spray! His luck held and he was pulled out alive and unhurt. He had had some second thoughts, however, according to a reporter who interviewed him after his feat.

He said that after he entered the river he weakened and would have given anything in the world if he could have reached terra firma once more. He attempted to get ashore by using his paddles, when the swift current swept him back and turned his feet toward the brink of the cataract. When he saw that it was impossible to get out, he felt the same as a man that has to meet death, and he prayed for dear life. Just as he came to the brink of the falls he became unconscious through fright and remained so until he struck the water, churned into foam at the base of the falls, when he was temporarily brought to by the force with which he struck. Then he again lost consciousness and knew no more until he found himself lying in his rubber suit at the water's edge.

This adventure also landed Brodie in the lockup on a charge of attempted suicide. He, of course, denied this and said he went over the falls to prove it could be done. The magistrate, apparently sensing a way out, said he didn't believe Brodie went over the falls, and if he would just say so, he would be let off. Brodie promptly stated that he hadn't gone over the falls and started to walk out. But the judge wanted a signed affidavit to that effect. Brodie refused, saying that he was a Catholic and because of his religion could not perjure himself. It ended by his being turned loose on a one-year probation with a promise from the court that if he did it again his fine would be $500.

Brodie also took time off from pub-keeping to go on the stage. In February 1892, he appeared for a week in a Broadway perennial called *Money Mad,* a melodrama which happened to have a bridge among its props. There was great applause as Steve made a perilous leap—of three feet. In September 1894, the Fourteenth Street Theater presented *On the Bowery,* a play of sorts written especially for Brodie and staged largely in a facsimile of his beer emporium. The climax came in a scene high on a walkway of the Brooklyn Bridge. As two thugs hired by the villain tossed the heroine into the murky waters below, none other than the great Steve Brodie made the suicidal leap to save her.

HE SAID "GOODBYE" TO THE "HELLO GIRL"

That bathroom essential known to the British as the "WC" was invented by a London watchmaker. The first fully automatic machine for making straight pins, heads and all, was the brainchild of a New York City physician. So perhaps it is not too surprising that an undertaker in Kansas City, Missouri, was the inventor of a device used to switch telephone calls automatically—a system that evolved into the dialing and musical-tone pushbutton methods in use today, a system that eliminated "the voice with a smile," as the telephone ads in the old days described the girl in the central office.

This little-known inventor, who could properly be called the forgotten man of the communications industry, was Almon Brown Strowger, born in 1839 in Penfield, New York. He served three years in the Union army, then taught school in New York, Illinois and Kansas before entering the undertaking profession. The story goes that in 1886, just nine years after the first commercial telephone exchange was implemented, mortician Strowger became annoyed at the telephone service he was getting. He was losing trade, he believed, either because his calls were not being put through properly or because a competitor was bribing an operator to divert them. In any event, with little

or no knowledge of matters electrical, Strowger began looking for a way to make telephone service fully automatic.

Like many great inventions, Strowger's automatic telephone exchange device was relatively simple. It used electromagnets to activate a mechanism that moved a metal finger over a bank of contacts, each contact connected to a different telephone. The caller directed this metal finger to the right spot by pushing buttons at his or her end of the line. For instance, to reach a person whose number was 46, the caller pushed one button four times, another six times, then turned a crank to ring the bell at the other end of the line. To accomplish all this, five connecting wires were needed.

Having worked all this out and obtained patent protection, Strowger now had to promote his invention. Luckily he had contact with a venturesome salesman, Joseph Harris, who foresaw a future for the new device. The two opened a manufacturing plant in Chicago and hired a very experienced electrician from Baltimore, A. E. Keith, who believed in the device and became one of the founding members of the Strowger Automatic Telephone Exchange.

A golden opportunity for the fledgling corporation came when the local phone company in La Porte, Indiana, became involved in a patent infringement suit that ended with a judge ordering all of La Porte's telephones destroyed. A franchise was obtained from the city of La Porte and within a few months 250 of the city's residents were contentedly pushing buttons instead of bawling out the operator. On November 3, 1892, Strowger proudly showed off his revolutionary setup to a large group of interested people who had answered his invitation. Telephone owners had been forewarned and were asked to answer their phones very promptly if they rang between 12:30 and 4 p.m., the hours of the demonstration. The system worked well and received very favorable reviews by reporters. The Strowger Automatic System became known as the "girl-less, cuss-less, out-of-order-less, wait-less telephone."

Strowger's new system was gradually extended to many other cities, largely in the Midwest. Along the way, the company's engineers came up with another notable advance in telephony—the finger wheel dial, which was easier than counting as one pushed buttons on the earlier phones. The first dial phones were installed at Albion, New York in 1896.

Before the turn of the century, the automatic telephone exchange had migrated across the Atlantic with a 200-line installation in London and one double that size in Berlin. During the Spanish-American War, an automatic exchange was installed in the White House, connecting President William McKinley with the offices of his cabinet members without any third parties being able to listen in at a central office.

The Automatic Electric Co. was formed in 1901 and acquired the manufacturing rights from the Strowger Automatic Telephone exchange. The Strowger company held the patent rights until 1908 when Automatic Electric acquired the stock. "Ma" Bell first used the system in 1918 when an order was placed for an 11,000-line exchange for Norfolk, Virginia. In 1919 the Bell System officially announced its intention to adopt dial switching on a progressive basis. Today the great majority of the telephones in the United States are served by dial equipment.

Globe Trotting Nellie Bly

I hold here in my hand a lengthy ca-ble-gram, That came from
far a-cross the sea— It's from Miss Nellie Bly, and its contents I will
try to tell if you will listen unto me— She's trying very hard to beat the
world's re-cord to round the world in sev-en-ty five days— Of the many
funny sights in her ca-ble-gram she writes, of the people and their very
curious ways— With an um-brel-la and a grip, she gave her friends the
slip, far a-cross the deep blue sea; It was a pleasant trip for her
grip was not "La Grippe", con-se-quent-ly she was happy as could be—

OUR NELLIE MADE IT

As the band struck up an old Stephen Foster melody, the crowd that packed Jersey City's railroad station broke into a roar. A slip of a girl, dressed in a fashionably cut ulster, wearing a newsboy cap, and carrying a monkey on her shoulder, stepped from the train onto a red carpet.

All the fuss was over 22-year-old Nellie Bly, feature reporter for Joseph Pulitzer's New York *World,* who had just finished circumnavigating the globe in 72 days, 6 hours and 11 minutes, thereby breaking the 80-day record of Jules Verne's fictional hero, Phileas Fogg.

Nellie Bly, born Elizabeth Cochran, had earned quite a reputation as a reporter despite her youth. It started when she answered a *Pittsburgh Dispatch* editorial, entitled "What Girls Are Good For," that opposed woman suffrage and criticized women who sought careers outside the home. The fiery reply she sent to the *Dispatch* got her her first newspaper job, and under the nom de plume Nellie Bly she began a career as an investigative reporter. Nellie Bly's forte was exposing social ills—life in the slums, unfair

121

working conditions, the poor lot of the working girl and the desperate existence of inmates in Pittsburgh's jails.

The *Dispatch* sent Nellie to Mexico to report on government corruption and living conditions of the poor contrasted with those of the rich. Her stories made her unpopular with the Mexican government and she was soon asked to return to the United States.

In 1887 the undaunted reporter went to New York, determined to join the staff of the New York *World,* and was able to make a deal with Joseph Pulitzer: in return for a job with the *World* she would deliver a hot news story on the horrid conditions under which the mentally ill were forced to live. To do this she faked an attack of insanity at a boarding house she had checked into earlier in the day and was shortly on her way to the insane asylum on Blackwell's Island. The nightmarish stories she came back with were enough to horrify readers across the country and result in extensive reform.

Disguising herself so as to obtain inside information became Nellie's *modus operandi.* With the *World* protecting her identity she was able to expose many injustices, and her stories prompted investigations into several fraudulent business practices.

But the highlight of Nellie's career—her trip around the world—was a departure from this format and content. When she first suggested the idea, prompted by the popularity of Jules Verne's *Around the World in Eighty Days,* Pulitzer was unimpressed. But he was finally persuaded, and on November 14, 1889, Nellie set out for England by steamer. She traveled light, her luggage consisting of a small suitcase and a bulging shoulder bag. On short notice a fashionable New York tailor had created the costume that was to be her trademark.

With one exception, the route followed by the now famous reporter was much the same as that taken by the hero of Jules Verne's novel; Nellie omitted Phileas Fogg's adventure-filled rail trip across India.

From England she crossed the channel to France, where she interviewed author Jules Verne. From France her itinerary took her by train to Brindisi, on the heel of Italy's boot. The remainder of the voyage was traveled via a succession of steamers—through the Suez to Ceylon, thence to Singapore, Hong Kong, Yokohama, and the Golden Gate. At San Francisco a special train waited for her.

Nellie sent back lengthy cables describing her experiences, the people she met, the intriguing items she saw in the shops of the Orient. Her readers seemed to love it. For them Nellie embodied the romance of journalism and good old American spunk. The *World* invented a parlor game called "Around the World with Nellie Bly," and initiated an extremely popular contest in which participants filled in coupons from the paper with their guesses as to the actual time the trip would require. Many other papers all over the country followed Nellie's progress and were permitted to print the contest coupons.

For Nellie it wasn't all roses. There were anxious moments: when the train to Brindisi lost two hours, when the ship from Yokohama to San Francisco encountered storms about as bad as they come. And at San Francisco Nellie learned that the direct rail route east was blocked by snow in the Sierras.

But, luckily, at Brindisi the ship waited for the train. In the Pacific the steamer rode out the storms. In the States her special train was rerouted southward through Arizona and New Mexico. Through the Western plains her luck was better than Phileas Fogg's. His train was attacked by Indians and slowed down for hours by migrating buffalo; when Nellie came along the Indians were on reservations, the buffalo gone.

There was one bad time in the Far East, when Nellie learned that another woman writer, Elizabeth Bisland of *Cosmopolitan* magazine, was circling the globe in a westerly direction, attempting to beat her time. She needn't have worried. Miss Bisland's attempt somehow failed to stir up any excitement.

For the duration of Nellie's trip the *World* made her front page news, and her arrival in Jersey City on January 25, 1890, was signaled with factory whistles, waving flags and cheering throngs. She had beaten Phileas Fogg's record with time to spare and she was a national heroine.

BIG WHEEL

The conventional Ferris wheel one sees at a carnival or county fair today stands about 50 feet high and has 12 to 16 two-passenger seats. But the one which gave these popular amusement park attractions their name was a truly extraordinary engineering feat of much grander proportions, created especially for the 1893 World's Columbian Exposition at Chicago.

Impressed by the popularity of the new 984-foot-high Eiffel Tower at the Paris Exposition of 1889, the construction chief of the Chicago exposition challenged America's civil engineers to come up with something as unique and daring as the creation of Alexandre Gustav Eiffel, and, of course, something that would generate publicity and bring droves of visitors to Chicago.

George Washington Gale Ferris, a 33-year-old Pittsburgh bridge builder, accepted the challenge and submitted a design for a giant revolving wheel with passenger cars. His ambitious plans specified a wheel of 250 feet in diameter having 36 cars, *each* with a capacity of 60 people. Filled, the giant wheel would carry 2,160 people at once.

At first Ferris was laughed at, but he persisted with promoting his idea, and although the country was in a depression he managed to raise enough money to finance the Ferris Wheel Company. However, it was not until mid-December 1892, only about four months before the exposition's gates were to open, that a contract was signed and construction began. Ferris was to retain the first $300,000 and split the additional profits with the exposition.

Since no single mill or machine shop could possibly have handled a project of such magnitude in the time available, Ferris farmed out the work to a number of companies. Relatively few parts could be assembled until they were on the construction site, so the greatest precision was necessary; the slightest error could prove disastrous.

In mid-March the 45-foot-long axle which would turn the wheel arrived in Chicago from Pittsburgh, where it had been forged. Various other parts began to come in from the many companies Ferris had contracted, and ironworkers labored daily throughout the spring.

Finally, on June 9, the wheel was powered to make its initial, carless test run. Workers were stationed at various strategic (and potentially dangerous) points. All watched with held breath as the tremendous structure began to move. Miraculously, the wheel turned without a groan. Then came the job of hanging the 36 cars, each having five large plate glass windows on each side.

The wheel was ready to carry passengers on June 21, seven weeks after the opening of the exposition. From the beginning fair-goers flocked to it, regardless of the weather. Many seemed more interested in the novelty of the wheel itself than in the unparalleled view of Chicago and Lake Michigan it afforded on clear days. At night the structural steel giant was illuminated by 3,000 of Thomas Edison's new incandescent lamps. Loading and unloading of the cars was facilitated by the use of six platforms. A ride consisted of two revolutions of the wheel. On the first, six stops were made for loading. The second was a nine-minute nonstop journey through the sky.

125

Even though it had to compete with another famous Midway attraction, the belly-dancer "Little Egypt," and with Buffalo Bill's "Wild West" staged just outside the exposition grounds, the Ferris Wheel was the talk of Chicago. Thanks to excellent design and meticulous construction, it enjoyed four months of trouble-free operation. And it made money for everyone concerned. When the exposition closed in early November 1893, one and a half million customers had had a bird's-eye view of Chicago and Lake Michigan on the most thrilling amusement park ride in history.

The success and popularity of the wheel was cut short after the Chicago stint. In the spring of 1894, Ferris' wheel was to be shipped to New York for erection at 37th Street and Broadway, but the plan fell through. After nearly a year of being dismantled and in storage on railroad cars in the Chicago area, the wheel was finally reassembled at an amusement park adjacent to Lincoln Park in Chicago.

Visions of large crowds and profits did not become reality and the attraction closed. It remained standing until 1904 and after being bought at public auction for a mere $1,800 it was moved to St. Louis for the Louisiana Purchase Exposition.

The Ferris Wheel was popular at the exposition, but due to the high transportation and reerection costs the profit realized was small. At the close of the event it was left again, as it had been in Chicago, to become an eyesore. In May of 1906 the wheel was sold to a wrecking company and dismantled for the last time—with 200 pounds of dynamite.

The end of Ferris' original wheel was not to be the end of the "World's Greatest Ride." Even while the giant wheel was the talk of two continents and was towering over two expositions, experimenters the world over were trying to duplicate and improve upon Ferris' initial conception.

Although many of these pioneers were European, one, W.E. Sullivan, a Chicago bridge builder, decided to build smaller portable wheels modeled after Ferris'. In 1906 Sullivan went on to found the Big Eli Bridge Co.,which to this day manufactures most of the Ferris wheels operating in amusement parks and carnivals.

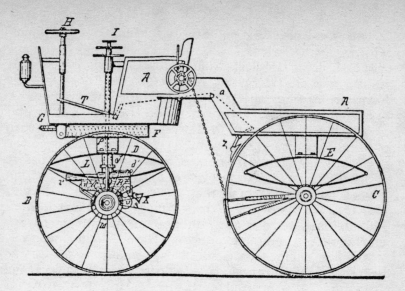

HENRY BLEW THE WHISTLE

An antique automobile built in 1905 from plans and specifications dating back to 1879 went on permanent display a few years ago among the buttons, firearms and clocks at the museum of the Connecticut State Library in Hartford. Its story is a fascinating footnote to the most bizarre chapter in the early annals of America's automotive industry—the Ford-Selden patent squabble, which dragged through the courts for eight years and, on the side, stirred up an advertising wrangle that has had few, if any, equals. The story behind the old car also recalls the period, a brief one to be sure, when New England was ahead of Detroit in the production of automobiles.

In 1895 the U.S. Commissioner of Patents granted a patent on a self-propelled road vehicle powered by an internal combustion engine. Did this prize package go to some noted automotive pioneer such as Ransom E. Olds, Alexander Winton, Henry Ford, or one of the Duryea brothers? No, but rather to a man who never in his life had built a car with his own hands.

The recipient of this potentially valuable piece of paper, which carried with it an implied monopoly on the manufacture and sale of gasoline-powered cars for 17 years, was 49-year-old George Baldwin Selden of Rochester, New York, an attorney specializing in patent law.

Selden had served short hitches in the Union army and at Yale before turning to the law. He had an inventive turn of mind and actually took out several patents prior to the one that was to make his name a household word for nearly a decade. Fascinated for years by internal combustion engines and the idea of a practical self-propelled road vehicle, in 1876 he went to the Centennial Exposition in Philadelphia to demonstrate one of his inventions, a machine for making barrel hoops. Here Selden saw a new stationary engine designed by an Englishman, George Brayton, which burned crude petroleum. Back home again, he experimented with engines intermittently for several years. Then he worked out, on paper, a way to install a lighter version of the Brayton engine in a "road wagon," and transmit power to the front wheels by means of a clutch and gearshift.

None of these—wagon, engine, clutch, gears—was new. But the thought of putting them together was then an innovation. Selden believed he had what the Patent Office would consider a new and useful machine. His patent application, submitted in the spring of 1879, read: "The object of my invention is a safe, simple, and cheap road locomotive, light in weight, easy to control, and possessed of sufficient power to overcome any ordinary inclination." As the Patent Office did not require a working model, all Selden had to do was submit a drawing and a description, in this case a drawing and a description of something that actually did not exist.

Selden had neither the mechanical skill nor the financial resources to attempt building and marketing such a contrivance himself. During the years that followed he tried repeatedly to interest others in helping develop his invention, but without success. Among those he discussed it with was George Eastman, one of his clients. He was just ahead of his time. However, with rare foresight he put himself in a position to be in on the ground floor if a demand for such vehicles ever materialized.

So long as no one was building a gasoline-powered "road locomotive," if Selden were granted a patent he would have only a piece of paper, and one that in 17 years could become worthless. But being a patent attorney he knew that by filing additional claims he could delay the issuance of the patent and still be protected. From time to time he filed such claims and thus kept the application open for 16 years. Then, with an uncanny sense of timing, he stopped filing and the patent was issued on November 5, 1895.

By 1895 the gasoline-powered car was no longer just a dream. In France the famous firm of Panhard & Levassor was turning out autos with the basic design still in use—front engine, clutch, gearshift and differential. All over the eastern United States "horseless carriages" were being put together by clever mechanics looking way down the road. On Thanksgiving Day, 1895, only a few weeks after the postman had delivered Selden's patent to him, America's first official auto race—really an endurance contest—was staged by the Chicago *Times Herald.* The startling total of 11 machines entered.[1] A new industry was on its way—up.

But although humming, the infant industry was composed largely of small-fry operators without solid financial resources. So Selden put away his piece of paper and occupied himself with his patent law practice. Strangely enough, it was an electric automobile, or rather the failure of one, that brought him to prominence a few years later.

Among those who believed that old dobbin had had it was wealthy and influential bicycle manufacturer Colonel Albert Pope of Hartford, Connecticut, who, in 1895, hired young inventor Hiram Percy Maxim to develop "horseless carriages" for the Pope Manufacturing Company. The Pope Company was the first going concern in the United States to put its resources and know-how behind the production of that newcomer to the transportation field, the automobile. But in spite of Maxim's deep personal in-

[1]For an account of the race, read *No Turkey For The Duryeas* on page 135.

terest in the gasoline car, Pope soon joined a group of New York promoters headed by William Whitney in a grandiose scheme to build an industrial empire founded on the electric taxicab. Even so, to be on the safe side, the syndicate approached Selden and opened negotiations for control of his patent. The result was that, in 1900, for $10,000 and a promise of future royalties, the Selden patent became one of the assets of the new Electric Vehicle Company, which bought Pope's auto manufacturing facilities.

Like Selden's "road wagon," Electric Vehicle looked good on paper. However, the company soon failed through gross mismanagement, which included questionable stock manipulations and a shady transaction involving a $2 million bank loan that became a public scandal. And the electric taxis were a dismal failure. In his book *Horseless Carriage Days,* Hiram Percy Maxim described their uninspiring career in New York City.

These vehicles had enormous storage batteries which weighed nearly a ton. These were removed every time the cab came in from a run, no matter how short it may have been. Great hydraulic machines pulled the batteries out, delivered them to a traveling crane, and pushed in a fresh battery. The cabs were subjected to the most atrocious abuse imaginable. It always seemed to me that the worst thugs who could be found on the pavements of New York were selected to operate them. I remember one of them confiding to me, with an evil leer, that the cab drivers could beat any plan the company devised to insure receiving all the money the drivers collected. Regardless of the sort of drivers they had, these cabs were doomed. The gasoline engine drove every one of them off the streets. Lighter weight, higher speed, lower first cost, and lower operating expense did the job.

With disaster lurking just around the corner, Electric Vehicle played its ace-in-the-hole. In an attempt to recoup, the management decided to use the Selden patent as a club for extracting tribute from the manufacturers of gasoline-propelled cars.

Alexander Winton, the most influential man in the new

automobile industry, was one of those picked for the dubious honor of being test-sued. He held out in the courts for two years but gave up when a number of smaller manufacturers capitulated and applied for licenses. The next step was the formation, in 1903, of the Association of Licensed Automobile Manufacturers. Its agreement, signed by most of the leading companies, required the payment of royalties and promised no end of trouble for anyone brash enough to sell a "gas buggy" not equipped with a little metal plate reading "Licensed under Selden Patent No. 549,160, Patented November 5, 1895."

At the start, members kicked in 1¼% of the retail price of each car (five years later this was reduced to eight-tenths of one percent). A heavy slice of the cake went to Electric Vehicle. There were lawyers, accountants, etc., to be paid, too, but there was some left for Selden. After all these years he began cashing in on his paper brainchild.

Among the loose ends to be pulled together after the formation of the Association of Licensed Automobile Manufacturers was a matter concerning Henry Ford, a rugged individualist who insisted on building and selling cars without paying the so-called "Selden tax." Less than a year went by before an infringement suit had been filed in the Federal Circuit Court in New York against Ford and several offenders of lesser note.

Henry Ford, after two unsuccessful tries at manufacturing passenger cars, had achieved fame by building racing cars and hiring a former daredevil bicycle racer named Barney Oldfield to put them through their paces, which included chalking up the then unheard of speed of a mile a minute. In the midst of the publicity attending Oldfield's exploits, the Michigan farm boy with a passion for machinery organized the Ford Motor Company. In the same year (1903), Ford sounded out the new association concerning membership and was given the brush-off. By those already on the inside, he was considered a fly-by-night, a mere "assembler" of cars.

That did it! The story goes that when Ford's products caught on with the public, the association quickly changed its mind. But it was too late. Ford was not changing his. He had decided to go it alone, and to hell with the association and its patents.

Looking back on it, what followed seems almost ludicrous. After filing of the action, advertisements appeared warning the public that buying an unlicensed car was asking for a lawsuit. Ford soon presented his side, which cast him in the role of the poor man's St. George out to slay the dragon of the greedy interests. When the association considered making an example of the owner of an imported Mercedes, also an unlicensed product, Ford announced he would guarantee his future customers against loss by issuing a bond with every new car. So strong was the public's faith in Mr. Ford that virtually nobody bothered to ask for the bond. Merchant prince John Wanamaker, who had taken on the Ford agencies in New York and Philadelphia, got into the act, too—on Ford's side, of course. One of his advertisements read: "When you buy a Ford from John Wanamaker you are guaranteed against any trouble with the Trust; that's all the insurance any man would want. We believe the Selden patent is worthless."

To forestall any attempt by Ford to claim in court that the car described in Selden's patent would not have worked anyway, Selden had one built, at Rochester, and a beautiful job of workmanship it was. Another, a much cruder version, was constructed in the shops of Electric Vehicle at Hartford under the direction of an engineer named Henry Cave. This is the car that, after many, many years in storage, has been refurbished and placed on display in Connecticut's capital city.

Both machines constructed from the original drawings worked, after a fashion, with much coughing and sputtering. Neither could have won a race against a husky kindergartner on a tricycle, but they did move under their own power. The Rochester model had the numbers 1877 tacked on it when the inventor was put in it to be photographed, a liberty that has had many a caption writer scratching his head. This was the year in which Selden presumably made the drawings submitted with his patent application of 1879.

All this frenzied building of obsolete machinery doubtless helped the association's cause. When the case came to trial in 1909, six years after the suit was filed and a year after Ford brought out his famed Model T, the association and Selden won. In the eyes of the law the Selden patent was valid and Henry Ford was an infringer. Meanwhile, Electric Vehicle failed in the panic of 1907.

Ford lost no time in appealing, and the advertising war went on, with the public continuing to show its faith in Ford by grabbing his "Tin Lizzies" as fast as they came off the assembly line. Two years later the appellate court declared Ford the winner, in a decision worthy of Solomon. It ruled that the Selden patent was still valid but since Ford was not using a Brayton-type engine he was in the clear. At this point, with the patent having less than two years to run, the association called it quits. From then on, nobody paid royalties to anybody. Selden's patent documents were now good for nothing but papering the wall.

Selden at one time even went into the automobile manufacturing business himself. In 1906 he organized the Selden Motor Vehicle Company, which obtained a license and paid royalties to build cars under the Selden patent. Needless to say, his product had no relation to his drawings of 1877. Selden cars were produced until 1914. He also invested heavily in the Selden Motor Truck Company. With its dissolution in 1929, seven years after his death at the age of 77, George Baldwin Selden's name faded from the roster of the automobile industry.

In 1963 he was in the papers again, in small print and not without a touch of irony. Stevens Institute of Technology at Hoboken, New Jersey, custodian of the exhibits used in the Ford-Selden patent fight, presented the Selden-Rochester car, the one with the misleading 1877 tacked on its side and rear, to the Henry Ford Museum at Dearborn, Michigan. Now that the other car is being exhibited at Hartford after 60-odd years in storage, the final footnote appears to have been added to the Selden story.

Like so much of the other early history of the "horseless carriage," the record is blurry on just how much "the father of the automobile," as Selden called himself, actually collected during the eight-year productive life of his patent. His scholarly biographer William Greenleaf (*Monopoly on Wheels,* Wayne State University Press, 1961) chooses to believe his total take from royalties was $200,000. "It was a bountiful harvest," says Greenleaf, "for a patent finally adjudged as completely devoid of commercial value," which is no doubt true. However, considering all the abuse and ridicule directed against him, one might argue that Selden almost earned the money. One might add, too, that $200,000 seems rather "small potatoes" alongside the $5,800,000 Greenleaf says is an authoritative estimate of the total amount contributed by the auto manufacturers to the association's royalty pool.

Henry Ford's Model T put America on wheels and it and the multitude of other models produced by Ford's competitors became the whimsical subject of jokes, both critical and complimentary, by wags throughout the country. Here are just a few:

A man about to die had one death-bed request. He asked that his Ford be buried with him, because he had never been in a hole yet where his Ford didn't get him out.

"Why is Henry Ford a better evangelist than Billy Sunday?"
"Because he has shaken the hell out of more people than Billy Sunday ever saw."

"I simply can't stand the toot of an auto horn."
"Why not?"
"A fellow whom I hired as a chauffeur stole my automobile and eloped with my wife. Now every time I hear a horn toot I think he is bringing her back."

NO TURKEY FOR THE DURYEAS

When Frederick Adams, an employee of the Chicago *Times-Herald,* announced that a 54-mile horseless carriage race was to begin in Chicago on July 4, 1895, would-be inventors and self-taught mechanics headed for their basements, garages and shops to assemble their entries. Earlier in that year, the 87-mile Paris-Rouen race ignited a spark of interest in the horseless carriage among Europeans, and inspired Adams to follow suit with a well-publicized campaign.

H. H. Kohlsaat, new owner of the *Times-Herald,* was impressed enough by Adams' idea that he put up $5,000 in prize money, hoping the publicity would increase the circulation of his paper. A grand prize of $2,000 would go to the winner, the remaining $3,000 to be divided by the runners-up.

Adams stumped through the country like an overzealous politician running for high office, touting the great event for months. Support for his venture was given further impetus when the 700-mile Paris-Bordeaux-and-return race in June 1895 was heavily covered in the press. It was enough to garner over eighty entries, at least on paper, in the round trip Chicago-Evanston race. Since many of the entries under construction could not be completed by July, the race had to be rescheduled for Thanksgiving Day.

After returning home from his long drawn out campaign, Adams was confident that what started out as an idea would come finally to fruition. Unfortunately, the weather was not in his favor. His apprehension began to mount steadily when snow blanketed the city just three days before the race. Of the original number who agreed to take part, only eleven contestants now promised Adams to show up at starting time. Adverse weather conditions, however, prevented five from making their appearance at 8:30 a.m. at Jackson Park and Midway Plaisance.

A few days prior to Thanksgiving of 1895, youthful inventor Hiram Percy Maxim alighted from a train in

Chicago. Hired only four months before by the new motor carriage division of the famous Pope bicycle works at Hartford, Connecticut, Maxim came to the Windy City to witness America's first scheduled automobile race and, incidentally, to check on bicycle tycoon Albert Pope's potential competition in the untried automotive field.

All during November, strange-looking, self-propelled contraptions had been arriving in Chicago, sputtering through the streets, emitting foul odors and horrible sounds, frightening horses and citizens. In his memoirs, *Horseless Carriage Days,* published shortly after his death in 1936, Maxim gave his recollection of the hectic scene:

When I arrived in Chicago I found the most astounding assortment of mechanical monstrosities scattered around in various places in the city. The headquarters was a large race track several miles south of the center of the city, selected because it gave various entrants an opportunity to run their machines and tinker with them. This opportunity for tinkering was important because every machine needed about five hours of tinkering for every hour of running.

Fully fifty per cent of the entrants had not been able to get to the track. Downtown spaces had been provided for them. In all these spaces tired, harried, and extremely dirty men spent days and nights underneath or half inside these vehicles. There was everything from a bicycle with a direct connected crank from a gasoline cylinder on each side to immense wagons which seemed to have no definite system of propulsion.

Charles and Frank Duryea from Springfield, Massachusetts, were there with the best-looking outfit of all. It was a regular horse buggy. It had a two-cylinder engine in the back of the buggy body. The Duryea brothers were not anxious to exhibit this engine. The cover was kept down and very few, if any, were permitted to see what was inside. The carriage would run very well and needed less tinkering than any.

The German Benz carriage looked very queer with its belt drive. The belt was slackened and allowed to slip when it was desired to unclutch the engine from the carriage. But although the Benz looked like a machine shop on wheels, it gave a better account of itself than any of us believed it would.

On the morning of the race at Jackson Park, the starting judge gave the signal. The Duryea motor wagon, incidentally employing the first set of pneumatic tires ever used on an automobile, was the first car to take the lead. The other five trailed behind at a rather desultory pace. Frank Duryea maintained his lead, however, for only six miles when the steering column snapped. As he hurriedly spent an hour trying to repair it, a German Benz driven by Jerry O'Connor forged ahead. O'Connor's good fortune quickly turned sour on him when he hit a streetcar. His car was not seriously damaged until he later collided with a horse-drawn cab. Meanwhile, Duryea managed to regain his lead when O'Connor's vehicular difficulties eventually forced him out of the race.

Duryea finally made it to the finish line in what turned out to be more an endurance contest than a race. A second German Benz, the only other entry to complete the grueling run, came in several hours later. It crossed the finish line piloted by another noted American auto pioneer, Charles Brady King of Detroit, who was riding as umpire but took over when the official driver, Oscar Mueller, gave up from exhaustion.

While Chicagoans enjoyed their Thanksgiving feasts in the cozy warmth of their homes, Frank Duryea spent a long, frigid day at the tiller of his high-wheeled open-air vehicle, with his umpire, Arthur White, shivering beside him. It took them all of 10 hours and 23 minutes to cover the snow-drifted, fifty-four mile course. This included getting lost a few times and making several lengthy stops for repairs. Charles Duryea also made the trip in a horse-drawn sleigh, keeping in close touch with his younger brother and lending a hand in emergencies. As for Mr. Adams, the promoter of the first auto race, he became a forgotten man in the excitement, a footnote to a well-orchestrated event.

Hiram Maxim, who had been appointed an umpire and assigned to one of the two electrics, had an easy day. His driver dropped out of the race even before reaching the first of a number of relay stations where replacement batteries were stored.

It is curious to note that just a year after Duryea's triumph, another race was held in Narragansett Park, a Rhode Island horse racing track, where as a special attraction the horse was pitted against the machine. The chugging horseless carriages were hooted and howled at, and the classic imperative "Get A Horse!" was coined by some members of the crowd in attendance.

As the years witnessed greater strides in racing and the development of the automobile, fewer and fewer people turned a good ear to that arrogant claim of equine superiority. Indeed, the Duryea brothers lost no time in capitalizing on their hard-won success at Chicago and their favorable publicity. On returning to Springfield, they soon had their little factory humming. In fact, they became the first in America to manufacture automobiles for sale to the public. And for a year or so they had the field all to themselves. In striking contrast to the millions of cars now turned out annually by U.S. automakers, in 1896 the Duryea Motor Wagon plant produced a total of thirteen "gasoline buggies," all identical. The flamboyant showman P. T. Barnum, always on the lookout for new and interesting attractions, considerably enhanced the Duryeas' reputation when he bought one of their cars and featured it in his circus parades.

Only one of these 1896 Duryea cars has survived. Reconditioned in 1905 by Frank Duryea, it has been on display in the Henry Ford Museum at Dearborn, Michigan since 1972. Rather oddly, this car carries the serial number 37. Frank Duryea once explained to a former owner of the car, George H. Waterman, Jr., of East Greenwich, Rhode Island, that this was done to prevent snoopers from finding out just how many cars the fledgling Duryea factory at Springfield was building.

Competitors soon appeared in other parts of New England. In 1897 the bearded Stanley twins from Maine began producing their famous steamers at Newton, Massachusetts. Concurrently, over the objections of Hiram Maxim who was an advocate of the gasoline auto, Pope's Hartford works produced an electric vehicle—a two-seater Columbia phaeton. It was not until 1898 that the Middle

West seriously challenged Yankee ingenuity in the auto industry. In that year, in Cleveland, Ohio, Alexander Winton unveiled the first passenger cars offered for public sale west of the Hudson River. In 1899 Detroit entered the automobile business with the opening of the Olds Motor Works.

Despite their initial glowing successes, the Duryea brothers quarreled and parted company after the Duryea Motor Wagon had been in production only two years. Charles tried unsuccessfully to manufacture cars in both Peoria, Illinois, and Reading, Pennsylvania. Until his death in 1938 he remained active as a consulting engineer and writer on automotive matters. Frank joined the J. Stevens Arms & Tool Company of Chicopee Falls, Massachusetts, which began producing automobiles in the early 1900's.

For a long period Frank Duryea was embroiled in a bitter controversy with his brother Charles over Frank's contribution to the early development of the gasoline automobile, although a majority of the patents taken out by the Duryeas were in Frank's name. But with the passing of time he achieved recognition as one of those who rightfully belong on the roll of honor of the imaginative mechanical geniuses who helped put the world on wheels. In 1948 the Smithsonian Institution gave Frank equal credit with his brother.

Frank Duryea's name was in the headlines long before the world ever heard of Henry Ford, Ransom E. Olds, Alexander Winton, and the other famous automotive pioneers, and he outlived them all. In 1959, at the age of eighty-nine, he attended a performance contest of vintage cars in New York, running up Fifth Avenue from Washington Square to Central Park. He glanced at the rear engine of one of his 1896 cars and said nostalgically: "It's like a dream to look at the old fellow." He passed away in February of 1967 in a Connecticut nursing home at the age of ninety-seven. In his obituary *The New York Times* reported the funeral service was held in Springfield, where the car was produced and where he lived for a quarter of a century until he retired.

WHEN FEATHERS WERE IN FASHION

Visitors to a score of ranches in Southern California or Arizona's Salt River Valley shortly after the turn of the century, witnessed a revolutionary new trend in farming. Instead of fat beef cattle grazing in the pastures, here were skinny-legged, rubbery-necked ostriches— hundreds and hundreds of them—munching alfalfa behind sturdy woven wire fences as high as a man's head.

Ostrich feathers had become extremely fashionable as adornment for women's hats and clothing, first in Paris, then in the United States, and the domestication of the world's largest bird had become a very profitable venture.

The plumage of the ostrich had long been prized for its beauty and gracefulness. From time immemorial the wild ostriches native to Africa and the Middle East had been hunted to satisfy human vanity. But around 1865 South Africans discovered they could domesticate this ancient, ungainly bird who cannot fly but who can run like the dickens (up to 40 miles an hour). Ostrich farms soon sprang up in the region adjacent to the Cape of Good Hope. As the feather supply grew, so did the demand in Europe and the Americas.

On September 12, 1882, a New York newspaper stated that in the New York market alone the feather trade had increased during the previous five years from about $500,000 to $5,000,000, and was giving employment to more than 5,000 people. The largest feather importer, who claimed he alone was bringing in $2,000,000 worth for the year, gave his opinion of what was causing the boom:

"The ladies are wearing more feathers on their bonnets and hats than formerly. Two or three years ago a single ostrich feather was thought to be sufficient for one hat, but now fashion demands at least a double plume, and in some cases as many as six or seven feathers for each hat." This did not take into account the demand for feather boas, feather fans, feather muffs, frilly negligee trimmings and also that lowly household item, the feather duster.

Ostrich farming had spread from South Africa to Argentina and had come to the attention of the alert U.S. consul in Buenos Aires, E. H. Baker. He wrote a lengthy paper to Washington on how to raise ostriches in the United States and, most important of all, the fabulous profits to be derived therefrom. The State Department issued his optimistic findings in a pamphlet in October 1882. Before anyone could worry about how to obtain ostriches from Africa or Argentina the next chapter of the story unfolded.

In November of 1882 a South African grower named Dr. Charles Sketchley turned up in New York with 22 adult ostriches. Sketchley announced that he proposed to organize an American ostrich-breeding company. This, of course, would eliminate the high import duties and the cost of shipping the feathers from Cape Colony.

With his birds housed in a building in Central Park to recuperate from their long sea voyage, Sketchley began spreading the word about the huge potential profits in ostrich farming. On November 28, in a speech before the American Institute Farmer's Club in New York, he stated that California, with a climate much like that of South Africa, seemed to him to be the best place in the country for feather production. Following his own advice, he soon loaded his troop, as ostrich farmers called their birds, onto railway cars and was on his way west. He was able to interest a veteran poultry raiser in Anaheim, California, Billie Frantz. Greatly impressed, Frantz sold stock to raise the money necessary to buy the birds, hired Sketchley as an adviser, and America's first ostrich farm was in business.

Not surprisingly, the exotic replacements for Frantz's ordinary varieties of barnyard fowl brought a lot of visitors to his ranch. An admission fee of 50 cents was charged, but from the management's point of view it wasn't worth it. In an interview with a reporter from the San Francisco *Examiner*, Sketchley complained of visitors trying to pull feathers from the birds, breaking locks on the incubator house and committing many other acts of vandalism. "When you ask me what are the greatest drawbacks I have met with," he said, "I must answer dogs and visitors, and perhaps the visitors are the worst."

Ostriches are attracted by bright objects. They retaliated against unmannerly sightseers by grabbing and swallowing jewelry and hat ornaments, even watches, chains, and diamond stickpins, a practice that led to more than one seriously embarrassing moment for the farm's owner. As for the dog problem, it was very real. Although the ostrich is a fast runner and can deliver a death-dealing kick with its two-toed foot, it apparently has trouble kicking anything under a few feet high. Dogs accompanying visitors to Frantz's ranch made the ostriches very edgy. With his birds already nervous and tired from traveling more than 20,000 miles, Frantz had to take stern measures. He posted large signs saying dogs would be shot. When visitors ignored his warnings, he took Old Betsy off the wall and let go with a few pot shots. Then he raised the admission price to $25. All this finally brought peace and quiet to the Anaheim farm, and the birds settled down in their new home. The first ostrich chick born in America pecked its way into the world on July 4, 1883.

Shortly thereafter the time arrived for "plucking" the parent ostriches. The word is a misnomer, because the plumes are not pulled from the bird's tail and wings, but are clipped off close to the skin. The remaining stumps soon dry up and fall out or are easily removed to make room for the next crop, to be harvested some eight or nine months later.

For this humbling experience the bird is coaxed into a plucking box or pen and a bag is dropped over its head. The man wielding the clippers is careful to stay to the rear or side of the victim. The ostrich can deliver its powerful kick only to the front, and considering the indignity to which it is being subjected, it would no doubt be happy to land a kick or two if given the opportunity.

When word got around that Frantz and Sketchley were selling feathers at good prices, the Southern California ostrich industry started to grow. Others began importing birds or bargaining for young Anaheim stock. The word got to South Africa, too, and the growers there easily persuaded their government to slap an export tax on each bird or egg that left Cape Town—$25 per egg, $500 per bird. For Frantz this meant that the selling price of his young stock soon rose to $450 per bird.

Among those who imported ostriches was Edwin Cawston, who chartered a sailing ship, fitted it with padded enclosures, and left Cape Town with fifty birds. While some died at sea, in Cawston's words "a goodly number survived the trip and were soon established in their new home in Southern California." The home he referred to was Cawston & Fox's Washington Garden, opened near Los Angeles in February of 1887. This was the predecessor of the famous Cawston Ostrich Farm in South Pasadena that eventually became the best known operation of its kind in the entire country and remained in business until 1935.

While most of those who remember the Cawston farm think of it as a weekend tourist attraction, with hungry birds swallowing whole oranges and trained ostriches pulling carts or carrying riders on their backs, in its heyday it was America's leader in feather production and the envy of its competitors. Cawston's elaborate 1909-10 catalogue boasted it was "the largest ostrich feather market west of New York," that the gorgeous plumes in its South

Pasadena exhibition sales room were valued at $50,000. The company also maintained a sales room in downtown Los Angeles and a large breeding farm, with 1,000 birds, at San Jacinto, seventy-five miles to the east.

Arizona's first ostrich chick was hatched in 1891, from stock obtained from the Cawston farm. Growth of the industry in the Salt River Valley was painfully slow at first, but in time the dry climate and irrigated alfalfa fields in the Phoenix region proved so ideal for ostrich raising that investors finally began to show an interest. By 1905 there was a real boom—six farms in operation. The largest was the Pan American farm at Cashion, six miles west of Phoenix. It claimed 1,000 mature feather producers.

What about the profits? In the 1905 Year Book of the U.S. Department of Agriculture, Watson Pickrell of Tempe, Arizona wrote: "An ostrich will yield annually one-and-one-half pounds of feathers, with an average value of $20 a pound." Not very big money when you consider that a whole acre of pasture planted to alfalfa was necessary to maintain four birds. However, the big profit, aviculturist Pickrell pointed out, was coming from the sale of chicks. He wrote that in 1903 he bought twenty-one pairs of breeding birds for $16,800, which is $800 per pair. Within two years he had sold $30,000 worth of their progeny. And, of course, he still had the parent birds. At the same time, a full grown cow, which consumed fifteen times the alfalfa needed for a mature ostrich, was worth only about $50. How could one lose on the ostriches?

As a fringe benefit, or possibly as a hedge against the day when the demand for chicks might slacken, Pickrell suggested that the ostrich grower who did not care to increase the size of his troop had a ready food supply in the 36 to 90 three-pound eggs produced annually by each female ostrich. Of course, in order to capitalize on this, one needed a large family and a king-size skillet.

Hot Springs, Arkansas, was the home of the largest U.S. ostrich farm outside Arizona and California. In 1899 Thomas A. Cockburn had shipped fifty birds from California to San Antonio, Texas. Two years later his advertising was featuring "McKinley, the largest ostrich in America, standing ten feet high and weighing 340 pounds." After only a few years in Texas, Cockburn moved to the Arkansas spa, where his over 300 birds and his feather shop remained an attraction for visitors for half a century. The star of the Cockburn troop was a handsome male ostrich named Black Diamond. Harnessed to a sulky, this unusual performer was put through his paces on Sunday afternoons on the farm's quarter-mile track. During state fairs held many years ago on the Oak Lawn Jockey Club grounds in Hot Springs, Black Diamond thrilled the crowds by competing in harness races against fast horses. Celebrities patronizing the famous spa's fashionable hotels often were treated to ostrich egg omelet suppers.

In 1911 an optimistic progress report on the fast-growing U.S. ostrich industry appeared in a circular issued by the U.S. Bureau of Animal Industry. A survey by the bureau indicated at least 6,100 breeding and feather-producing ostriches in the United States. The circular further stated that despite the growing domestic production of feathers, the demand was still so great that imports also continued to climb, regardless of duties of 20 percent on raw feathers and 60 percent on processed plumes. The future looked bright for ostrich farmers in the Southwest.

It did indeed until shortly after the start of World War I. Then all those optimists who had been buying and selling chicks discovered they had been living in a fool's paradise. Feathers suddenly went out of fashion. It was hard to believe at first, just as thirty years ago nobody would have believed that today the candidates for public office, even the highest office, would stand bareheaded in the sun, rain or snow to harangue the voters, also largely hatless. But it happened. Almost overnight the hitherto stylish bonnet sporting from one to seven ostrich plumes was gone. Some blamed it on the growing popularity of the automobile. Fluttering feathers hardly seemed a practical accessory to the costume of the early feminine motorist. More likely it was all brought about by a handful of fashion arbiters in Paris. Or perhaps it was just time for a change.

In any event, the ostrich farmers were caught square in the middle. Lovely feathers worth a fortune one day

145

became passé the next. Birds formerly valued at hundreds of dollars could be had by zoos and circuses for almost nothing. And despite Mr. Pickrell's suggestions, scrambled ostrich eggs never became a standard breakfast dish.

When Arizona's Pan American farm was closing down, Dr. A. J. Chandler, developer of the Arizona community named for him, bought one hundred of its birds, planning to exhibit them at Chandler as a publicity stunt. Unwise to the ways of his new pets, he sent six mounted cowboys to herd them from Cashion to their new home, a distance of about thirty-five miles. Nobody had told him nor the cowboys that ostriches lack the herding instinct of cattle and horses. As long as the route lay between fenced pastures, everything went well. But once the troop hit the open desert, its members bolted in all directions, and that was the last anyone saw of many of them.

The Cawston farm at South Pasadena, largely because of its location in the heavily populated Los Angeles area, managed to stay in the business of entertaining tourists until 1935. The Cockburn farm in Arkansas also survived, for much the same reason, until the 1950's. Most of the other ostrich farmers simply had to destroy many of their birds and then presumably were themselves drowned in red ink.

But the pioneering Billie Frantz survived. Even after living through the growing pains of the first few years at Anaheim, he still had plenty of problems with his cantankerous ostriches, even lost a large part of his troop in a stampede caused by a dog. But meanwhile farsighted Billie had been quietly converting his acreage to orange groves.

DR. JACKSON,
FIRST TRANSCONTINENTAL MOTORIST

In the spring of 1903 Dr. and Mrs. Horatio Nelson Jackson, well-to-do residents of Burlington, Vermont, visited San Francisco. At the University Club Dr. Jackson got into an argument over the reliability of that new-fangled invention commonly known as the "gasoline buggy." The general feeling was that nobody but a fool would venture very far from home in one of those noisy, smelly contraptions that were always breaking down. The visiting physician from Vermont took the opposite view. He championed the automobile. In fact, his opinions on the matter were so strong that he committed himself to the unheard-of task of driving one across the continent, from San Francisco to New York, just to prove he was right, and to collect a $50 bet.

Like the great English naval hero for whom he was named, thirty-one-year-old Dr. Jackson was a man of action. Probably with more than just a touch of luck, he was able, almost immediately, to purchase a nearly-new 2-

cylinder Winton auto and to engage a resourceful young mechanic named Sewall K. Crocker, who also was imbued with the pioneer spirit. The pair loaded down their vehicle, which they named the *Vermont,* with equipment they felt would be needed, including extra gasoline and oil containers, camping gear and a block and tackle. Within five days of the discussion at the University Club, Mrs. Jackson had returned home by train and the two adventurers were ready to face the unknown. They ran the *Vermont* up the gangplank of the Oakland ferry on May 23.

The car that was to carry Dr. Jackson and Sewall Crocker to fame in the annals of early automobiling was a two-seater with a small, open luggage compartment in the rear. As was common in those days, there was no top and no windshield. The 20-horsepower water-cooled engine, cranked from the side, was mounted crosswise under the left-hand seat, its power transmitted to the rear wheels by a clacking chain that, under the best circumstances, delivered a speed of close to 20 miles per hour. The radiator was under a wooden hood in front. Since the demountable rim had not yet come along, the 4-inch tire casings, with their inner tubes, were fitted directly to wooden-spoked wheels.

To anyone brought up in the era of superhighways, the idea of driving a car over narrow mountain pack trails and trackless prairies probably is incomprehensible. Just how many miles the *Vermont* traveled is in question because about two weeks out of San Francisco, the car and its device for measuring distances parted company. However, when Jackson's route is laid out on a modern road map, it seems to come to about 4,000 miles, which does not allow for getting lost once in a while or following all the kinks that have since been ironed out by modern roadbuilders. A contemporary Winton advertisement claimed that the *Vermont* traveled more than 5,000 miles. The trip did not bother Dr. Jackson, however. The problems ahead, in May of 1903, seemed like just so many challenges to him. At first he was worried about the deserts of Nevada and Utah but Jackson avoided them by taking the longer northerly route out of San Francisco.

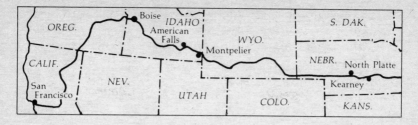

The first third of the trip was the most harrowing. Crossing the Sierras in northern California took its toll on the tires and countless time was spent scraping the inner tubes with the nutmeg grater, spreading glue, applying the patch, waiting for it to set and then heaving away at the pump. Fuel usually was to be had, but in lonely regions there were times when a long walk was necessary to obtain it. When the *Vermont* bogged down while crossing a streambed or in a king-size mudhole, the block and tackle usually got her back on dry land. But on occasions old-fashioned dobbin power had to be called in. Many rivers were crossed by bumping along railroad bridges hoping that a train would not show up. In places where there were no roads at all, these pioneer motorists did what seamen do—steered by compass.

After crossing the Sierras, Jackson went across the southeast part of Oregon and into southern Idaho, through Boise, American Falls and Montpelier. There was a humorous side to the trip, too. Upon entering Idaho, a white bulldog promptly named Bud, joined the expedition. Although he probably had never seen an automobile before, he took to motoring like a duck to water. When the dust began to bother his eyes, Bud was provided with a pair of goggles which he wore most of the way to New York.

After leaving Idaho and entering Wyoming, Jackson followed an eastward course that in general was much the same as today's Interstate Route 80. This part of the route across the plains went through Nebraska and its cities of North Platte, Kearney and Omaha; Iowa and its cities of Council Bluffs and Des Moines; and on into Chicago.

Jackson decided to take things easy east of Chicago. Instead of the shortest route of going over the Alleghenies in Pennsylvania, Jackson went the more level route through northern Indiana and Ohio, which goes along Lake Erie, and on through Buffalo, Albany and Poughkeepsie in New York.

The trip took Dr. Jackson and Crocker exactly nine weeks. However, not all of this time was spent on the road. There was time out for repairs and several long waits for parts or new tires to be sent by rail to the stranded motorists. Altogether, these unasked for waiting periods amounted to three weeks time. The trio of Jackson, Crocker and Bud arrived in New York City on July 26.

Winton's advertising was soon bragging about the way one of its stock models had stood up under the grueling cross-country run. Competitors immediately started a whispering campaign accusing the Vermont physician of having switched cars somewhere out West and also of having shipped his vehicle by rail around a few of the roughest spots. Winton capitalized on this by offering a $10,000 reward for proof of these tales. A later Winton advertisement stated that Dr. Jackson, upset by these attacks on his honor, was offering an additional $15,000 reward. Both Winton and Dr. Jackson were on safe ground. No claimants showed up, of course, but it all made good advertising copy.

When Dr. Jackson passed away in 1955, his obituary in *The New York Times* stated that his estimate of the cost of his trip was $8,000. Some would say that seems a hard way to collect a $50 bet.

Before he died, Dr. Jackson gave the *Vermont* to the Smithsonian Institution in Washington, D.C. In 1962 it was restored, given a fresh coat of red paint and placed on exhibition in the Institution's Museum of History and Technology.

HOW NOT TO MAKE A LAKE

Less than a century ago, in a certain valley in Southern California, there were no marinas nor opportunities for waterskiing, fishing, swimming or other water sports.

Today, however, the Salton Sea, California's largest inland body of water and a leading boating center in the state, stretches for 30 miles in the Imperial Valley where once only a 300-foot-below-sea-level depression was evident.

This lake was not made by nature but was a result of man's tampering with nature. The Salton Sea got where it is by a curious combination of circumstances—a miscalculation by promoters and the unpredictability of Mother Nature and her Colorado River—rather than by dam builders and hydraulic engineers. Once it was just the lowest portion of a sprawling dry area more than 100 miles long known as the Salton Sink.

In ages past, the sink had been a gigantic lake fed by the

waters of the mighty Colorado. But in time, the silt-laden river had built up a delta and natural levees that isolated the lake, leaving it to eventually dry up and become an awesome desert, though not the ordinary desert of sterile sand. The old lake bed was covered with fertile silt washed down from the vast regions drained by the 1,450-mile-long Colorado.

As far back as 1859, efforts had been made to nudge the state of California and Congress into a colossal irrigation scheme for the Salton Sink that was simplicity itself. This would have involved cutting the Colorado's high bank near the boundary with Mexico and letting the water run downhill to irrigate hundreds of thousands of acres that had the potential to be rich farmland.

But nothing happened, nothing but surveys and talk that is, for about forty years. Then in 1900, a private company, the California Development Company, was organized for the purpose of bringing Colorado River water to this arid region. Another, the Imperial Land Company, was formed for the purpose of attracting settlers and laying out town sites. The Salton Sink was rechristened with a more promotable name—Imperial Valley—and the reclamation work commenced.

Early in 1901 the west bank of the Colorado was cut on the California side five miles downstream from Yuma, Arizona. Water was diverted into a newly excavated, seven-mile canal paralleling the river and leading south to an ancient dry channel known as the Alamo River, which centuries earlier had carried the Colorado's water to the sink. This channel ran westward through Mexico for about forty miles before veering north into the Imperial Valley.

It all worked beautifully! Almost as though by the wave of a magic wand the precious life-giving liquid from the Colorado River was flowing into the valley's new irrigation ditches, 400 miles of them by the spring of 1902. Since the land belonged to the federal government and new settlers could file claims on large tracts by paying only nominal amounts of cash, the resulting boom was nearly the largest experienced by Southern California before or since. By 1904 some 79,000 acres were green with crops.

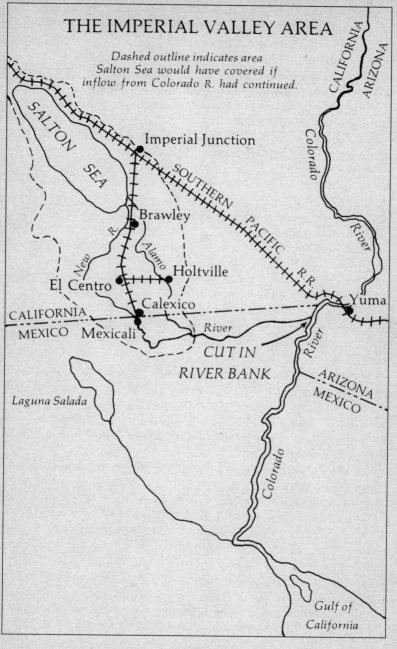

THE IMPERIAL VALLEY AREA

*Dashed outline indicates area
Salton Sea would have covered if
inflow from Colorado R. had continued.*

SALTON SEA

Imperial Junction

SOUTHERN PACIFIC R.R.

Brawley

Alamo

New R.

Holtville

El Centro

Calexico

CALIFORNIA

MEXICO   Mexicali

River

CUT IN
RIVER BANK

CALIFORNIA
ARIZONA

Colorado River

Yuma

River

ARIZONA
MEXICO

Laguna Salada

Colorado

Gulf of
California

But, in the fall of 1904, trouble came to Utopia. The seven-mile diversion canal had silted up badly, drastically reducing the amount of water that could be delivered to all the optimists who had been buying water rights in the valley. There was grumbling from the settlers and talk of lawsuits.

The developers quickly bypassed this hurdle and, eventually, brought disaster on themselves. A new cut was made in the Colorado's west bank in Mexico, about four miles south of the California boundary, and a new channel was scooped out a little more than half a mile long to connect with the old Alamo River bed. Plenty of water was again pouring into the parched fields. The valley's residents, now numbering more than 10,000, were jubilant.

The behavior of the lower Colorado had been fairly consistent during the quarter century that records had been kept. But unfortunately the great watercourse, as though in retaliation for man's intrusion, picked this particular time to misbehave and show its muscle. Beginning in February of 1905, before a gate had been installed across the new cut in the river bank, unprecedented floods rolled southward. The bank adjacent to the cut, formed primarily of silt almost as fine as ashes, began to crumble as the flood waters surged through the opening. By late summer, more than 90 percent of the Colorado's water was flowing toward the Salton Sink instead of following its usual course to the Gulf of California, tearing up valuable irrigation works on its way. The entire Imperial Valley was in serious danger of becoming a lake again.

Development company engineers made valiant efforts to repair the damage, only to see the results of their work washed away time and again by the angry river. The Salton Sink was filling up again. Railroad tracks were under water and green fields were being eaten away. By the end of 1905, it was apparent that only a near-miracle could save the Imperial Valley.

Miracles sometimes happen. When an appeal was made to railroad tycoon Edward H. Harriman, he accepted the challenge almost at once. True, his business interests were being affected as the rising waters lapped at the main transcontinental tracks of his Southern Pacific Railroad, and he faced the loss of receipts on produce being hauled from the valley by his freight cars. But whatever his motives, Harriman decided to plug the gap regardless of expense by sending in able engineers to do the job.

Two of Harriman's top men, Epes Randolph and Harry T. Cory, first tried conventional methods of fighting the river, but to no avail. The Colorado won every time. Then, while the surging flood waters continued to eat away at the river bank, Randolph and Cory evolved a daring plan that eventually worked. They decided that nothing would be able to turn the errant river back on the right track except a levee built of tons of solid rock. Engineer Cory thereupon opened his own quarries nearby and made arrangements to ship rock from other quarries as far away as Patagonia, Arizona (485 miles). He then built a nine-mile spur railroad to the levee construction site. Camps were set up for 2,000 laborers, many of whom were Indians, and various equipment including barges, pile drivers and steam shovels was assembled. The Mexican government, which also faced the dismal prospect of having a huge chunk of valuable real estate covered by water, cooperated by declaring martial law and supplying troops to police the labor camps.

Previous attempts at closing the break had narrowed the gap in the river bank to about 1,100 feet. To effect the final closure, two parallel wooden trestles about fifty feet apart were built on 90-foot pilings driven into the river bottom by pile drivers on barges. Immediately following the completion of the first trestle, late in January of 1907, long lines of heavily-loaded dump cars and flat cars that had been assembled on sidings began backing onto it and toppling tons of rock into the opening, a process that continued day and night for two weeks until the gap was closed. Even then the work did not stop. Many more trainloads of rock and gravel were added to the dam to make it secure. Then, to finish it off, the upstream side was covered with clay to make it impervious.

The excitement of the final scene of the drama was caught in the following description by F. H. Newell, director of the U.S. Reclamation Service, written for the 1907 annual report of the Smithsonian Institution.

The stones used were as large as could be handled or pushed from the flat cars by a gang of men, or by as many men as could get around a stone. In some cases the pieces were so large that it was necessary to break them by what are called "pop-shots" of dynamite laid upon a stone while it rested on the car. In this way the stones were broken and then could readily be thrown overboard by hand.

The scene at the closure of the break was exciting. Train after train with heavy locomotives came to the place and the stones, large and small, were pushed off by hundreds of workmen as rapidly as the cars could be placed. While waiting to get out on the trestle the larger stones were broken by "pop-shots," and the noise sounded like artillery in action. Added to the roar of the waters were the whistle signals, the orders to the men, and the bustle of an army working day and night to keep ahead of the rapid cutting of the stream.

On February 11, 1907, word was flashed to the world that the Colorado was conquered and the Imperial Valley saved. The effort had cost the Southern Pacific $3,000,000, not to mention the frequent disruption of the railroad's normal operations for months on end.

When it was all over, water covered an area about 45 miles long in the northern part of the valley. This gradually shrank through evaporation to the 30-mile-long saline water body with no outlet that we know today as the Salton Sea. Its water level (approximately 230 feet below sea level) remains fairly constant. Evaporation is offset by discharges from the present Imperial Valley irrigation system, which still gets its water from the Colorado River but by way of a modern dam and canal, both located on the California side of the border with Mexico.

As early as December of 1906, Edward H. Harriman had appealed to President Theodore Roosevelt suggesting that the federal government share in the expense of the rescue operation. The President encouraged Harriman to go ahead with the work but at the same time was vague about financial assistance. In 1908, with Roosevelt's support, a bill to partially reimburse the Southern Pacific was introduced in the House of Representatives. This got nowhere, even though the President's successor in the White House, William Howard Taft, realized the government's obligation and pushed hard for the legislation.

Harriman passed away in 1909 and the reimbursement bill died shortly thereafter. Later on, however, the Southern Pacific filed suit against the federal government. In the 1929 annual report of the company, Southern Pacific stockholders were no doubt pleased, and possibly amazed, to find the following item which wrote *finis* to one of the most exciting chapters in Southern California's history.

CLAIMS FOR CLOSING COLORADO RIVER BREAK

On page 22 of last year's report, mention was made of a suit brought under an Act of Congress, by your Company, in the Court of Claims, Washington, D.C., to enforce its claim against the Government of the United States, for the sum of $1,113,677.42, for expenditures incurred over twenty-two years ago, at the instance of President Roosevelt, in closing a break on the Colorado River to protect the Imperial Valley.

On April 12, 1928, United States Court of Claims Commissioner John M. Lewis filed his findings, allowing your Company, on account of its claim, the sum of $1,012,665.17. Government counsel, however, excepted to the findings of the Commissioner. Briefs were filed by your Company and by the Government and the case was orally argued before the U.S. Court of Claims in Washington, D.C., on February 5, 1929, and submitted to the Court for decision.

On June 10, 1929, the Court rendered a judgment in favor of your Company for the $1,012,665.17 awarded by the Commissioner. No appeal having been taken by the Government against the judgment, it became final on September 10, 1929, and the amount of the judgment was included in the "Deficiency Appropriation Bill" recently passed by Congress. On April 1, 1930, your Company received the Government's check for $1,012,665.17 in payment of the judgment.

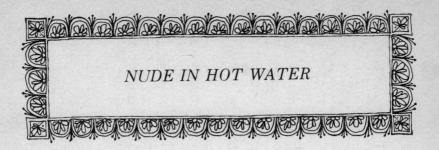

NUDE IN HOT WATER

An unemployed press agent, the secretary of the Society for the Suppression of Vice and a painting of a young girl about to skinny dip all joined forces to create a nationwide furor in 1913.

The painting, *September Morn,* by Paul Chabas, was unveiled in the Paris Salon of 1912. When reproductions went on sale the next year in New York, one appeared in an art store window on West 46th Street. It was brought to the attention of Anthony Comstock, the secretary of the Society for the Suppression of Vice, widely known as the scourge of gamblers, brothel owners and other evil doers, including artists who painted nude women. Enormously successful, Comstock credited himself with destroying 160 tons of obscene literature. However, he overestimated his prowess when he attempted to halt productions of George Bernard Shaw's play *Mrs. Warren's Profession.* Shaw's retaliation included the coining of the word Comstockery, which is defined as overzealous moral censorship of the fine arts and literature, often mistaking outspokenly honest works for salacious ones.

Comstock was noted for his furious raids. Publishers, gamblers and advertisers were all fair game. Few people could forget one of his appearances. Five-foot-ten, 210 lbs., invariably dressed in a black frock coat complete with a Bible in the pocket, Comstock would drive home an attack accentuated with blazing eyes flanked by muttonchop whiskers. When he walked into the 46th Street art store and ordered *September Morn* removed from the window, the clerk quickly obeyed. The proprietor, upon returning from lunch, promptly put it back, and the battle was on.

If a Hollywood press agent can be believed, Comstock was played for a sucker in *l'affaire September Morn*. In a posthumous autobiography, *Phantom Fame* (1931), Harry Reichenbach, who was widely known for his bizarre publicity stunts on behalf of the movie industry, related how as a young man down on his luck he spotted the picture in the window of the New York art store. He talked the proprietor into promising him $45, a month's rent, in return for a promotional stunt which would dispose of the store's large stock of prints, then going begging at ten cents each.

Reichenbach said he phoned Comstock several times, protesting the window display. When Anthony refused to bite, Reichenbach went to his office and personally escorted him to the scene of the crime. There the pair found a group of urchins, hired by the wily press agent, gesticulating and grimacing in front of the picture. The great reformer went to work, and *The New York Times* obligingly ran just the headline Reichenbach needed: COMSTOCK DOOMS SEPTEMBER MORNING.

In the ensuing uproar the American public was treated to one of the hottest controversies over morals, art and nudity ever to hit the front pages of the newspapers. The publicity naturally sold vast quantities of prints, calendars, cigar bands, candy boxes, and umbrella and cane heads, all bearing the young lady's undraped figure. Sailors had the young miss tattoed on their chests and tavern keepers even had replicas drawn on their barroom floors. Everyone was happy but Anthony Comstock.

September Morn made its most recent appearance in *The New York Times* on September 1, 1957. This time there were no blaring headlines, instead a brief item which began "With age comes respectability." The article went on to say that the Metropolitan Museum of Art had acquired the painting, more as an historical curiosity than as a representative of significant art. It is doubtful that, without the aid of Anthony Comstock, Paul Chabas' *September Morn* could ever have hung in the Great Hall of the museum.

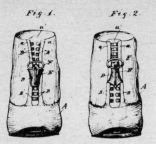

THE ZIPPER,

A TWENTY-YEAR SLEEPER

Ralph Waldo Emerson predicted that the world would beat a path to the door of the man who could build a better mousetrap. For many inventions Emerson's prediction was easily confirmed. Two years after Alexander Graham Bell first exhibited his telephone at the Centennial Exposition in Philadelphia in 1876, the first telephone exchange was put into operation at New Haven, Connecticut. Nylon thread, perfected in 1938, was being widely used in women's stockings by 1940. Within a few years after King C. Gillette designed the throwaway blade for the safety razor, his sales curve began running off the top of his charts.

But progress in making a discovery or perfecting an invention often proceeds at a rather slow and laborious pace. Moreover, public acceptance is not always immediate. The toothed zipper was perfected in 1913, but twenty years elapsed before it came into widespread use.

Credit for being the first to conceive of the idea of a slide fastener belongs to an energetic Chicago inventor named Whitcomb L. Judson. In 1893 he was granted a patent on a device described by him as a "clasp locker or unlocker for automatically engaging and disengaging an entire series of clasps by a single continuous movement." Judson's invention was based on what could be called the "hook and eye" principle. It consisted of two chains, each made with alternate links and hooks. As a slider was moved over the chains, the hooks on one chain engaged the links of the other, and vice versa, making the closure. Unlike the modern zipper, which is attached to tapes, the Judson fastener was designed to be laced into the high shoes worn by both men and women at the time. Unfortunately, it was clumsy and it never worked smoothly. Years later he refined it by placing all the hooks on one side of the fastener, all the eyes on the other, and clamping them onto tapes. The result—put on the market in 1905 as the C-Curity Placket Fastener—was only a slight improvement. The trade name promised too much. At this stage in its development, the slide fastener was not all that "C-Cure," as many women found out to their embarrassment.

Along the way, Judson's path had crossed that of Colonel Lewis Walker of Meadville, Pennsylvania, a lawyer and National Guard officer, who became intrigued with the slide fastener. Walker believed in its future and he soon was devoting much of his time and money to make it a workable product. He formed the Automatic Hook and Eye Co. of Hoboken, New Jersey, which offered Judson's C-Curity fastener to the American consumer.

Problems subsequently developed with the new fastener, bringing Walker and his associates to the realization of a need for the services of a highly trained mechanical engineer. They found their man in the person of Swedish-born Gideon Sundback, who had crossed the Atlantic in 1905 to work for the Westinghouse Electric Corporation in Pittsburgh, Pennsylvania. In 1906 Sundback signed on with the Hoboken plant. His first assignment was to perfect the Judson fastener.

Working diligently, he designed an improved version of the C-Curity Fastener, embodying the hook and eye principle. Given the name Plako, the fastener still had problems that kept it from becoming a big seller.

In 1913 Sundback took a fresh look at an old problem by putting aside every idea Judson had for the fastener. Meanwhile, the company had been reorganized under the name Hookless Fastener Co., and its rather miniscule manufacturing operation moved to Meadville in the northwestern part of Pennsylvania. After one unsuccessful try at producing an item Sundback called Hookless no.1, he came up with the solution in December of 1913. Dubbed Hookless no. 2, this was essentially the slide fastener most commonly used today. While it looked like a row of teeth, on close inspection it turned out to be a string of nested, cup-shaped members that interlocked, or unlocked, with a tug on the sliding clasp. The simple little members could be stamped out of metal in one process. Whitcomb L. Judson's complicated hook and eye principle had been abandoned.

Sundback still had to design and build precision machines for manufacturing the new product in quantity. But he and Colonel Walker at last had a winner; however, many years were to pass before they could be entirely sure of it. While they waited, because the struggling little Meadville company could not afford to pay the best of salaries, inventor Sundback received, as part of his compensation, foreign rights to the manufacture of slide fasteners.

Eventually, Plako became one of a hundred novelty items sold from door to door by peddlers, but Colonel Walker and his associates believed that Hookless no. 2 deserved a better fate. They decided to contact the clothing manufacturers, businessmen who could use the new product on a massive scale. But no matter how hard the company's salesmen worked, business did not improve. The clothing industry simply balked completely at the thought of changing its methods. Buttons continued to be sewn on men's trousers, hooks and eyes on women's dresses. As far as assistance from the public was concerned, people were not about to demand a product they had never even heard of in the first place.

During World War I the little factory at Meadville received quite a boost when a manufacturer of money

162

belts, sold chiefly to the U.S. Navy, whose uniforms were notoriously short on pockets, began calling for fasteners. His total order came to 24,000. A life preserver vest for the Navy also needed slide fasteners, 10,000 of them, and there were small orders from makers of specialized clothing of one sort or another. However, with the end of the war demand slackened considerably.

While Sundback spent time improving the machinery and Colonel Walker considered various methods of tapping the clothing market, the unexpected happened. In January of 1919, a young man appeared at the company's New York sales office with a tobacco pouch to which he had attached a slide fastener. He announced that he was entering the business of manufacturing his Locktite Tobacco Pouches. By 1922 he was putting a strain on the Meadville facilities by ordering 100 gross of fasteners per week.

In the same year actual expansion of the factory became necessary when the B. F. Goodrich Company, after a long period of experimentation, decided to put slide fasteners on a new line of stylish winter footwear to replace the ungainly, flopping galoshes then in vogue. Goodrich began by calling the new product the "Mystick Boot." The name failed to catch the public ear. Then Goodrich president Bertram C. Work coined the word "zipper" and in 1923 began advertising the "Zipper Boot." The catchy new name made a world of difference to both Goodrich and Hookless, and a new word had been added to the dictionaries.

Zippers soon began to appear on many articles of clothing—overalls, firemen's gear, golf jackets, women's girdles, flannel shirts, leggings—and on other items such as sleeping bags and covers for musical instruments. Nevertheless, the road to success with the men's clothing industry was still a rocky, uphill one. In 1929 the country fell into the worst depression of its history. No apparel maker was about to add the price of a zipper to a pair of pants when buttons cost only a few cents.

Applying a zipper to a pair of men's trousers was not an easy operation. Colonel Walker's problem was not just one of trying to peddle his better mousetrap. Entirely new methods for making trousers had to be worked out by Hookless engineers. Times did change, however, and finally two well-known Chicago houses placed small orders. In 1934 a Cincinnati firm began ordering 9,000 fasteners a week. In the summer of 1937 the Meadville factory suddenly found its phones ringing frantically and incoming mail and telegrams piling up. Men's clothing manufacturers all over the country had at last decided to adopt the little gadget en masse. Meadville went on three shifts and encountered many problems, but somehow they managed to weather the blizzard of new orders. Between 1932 and 1938 the number of large users of zippers for men's trousers increased from six to more than a thousand.

Cracking the women's dress market took a little longer. Nobody seemed to be in a hurry to replace the old-fashioned buttons, snaps or those difficult hooks and eyes. The campaign here posed special engineering problems, too. The zipper had to disappear into the dress. It could not catch on underclothing. In many cases it had to be able to withstand many washings.

In the late 1930's the women were barraged by a humorous advertising campaign with its most telling copy built around the coined word "Gap-osis." Some of the art work came from the pen of the gifted cartoonist James Thurber. "Does your dress have Gap-osis?" was often the line in ads which included drawings or photographs of women with unsightly apertures between their buttons, hooks or snaps. Nearly every well-groomed woman wished to avoid Gap-osis. The campaign was successful and the zipper for women's wear became a common feature of everyday apparel.

Colonel Lewis Walker and engineer-inventor Gideon Sundback lived to enjoy the benefits of their hard-won success. And, while many manufacturers today make zippers, Walker's Meadville plant, now known as the Talon Division of Textron, still turns out millions of those handy little gadgets with metal or plastic teeth or interlocking nylon coils.

CENT-A-GALLON GASOLINE

Genuine inventors have developed many extraordinary time-saving, cost-saving and energy-saving inventions throughout history. Some other inventors, at least calling themselves such, were, and are, responsible for seeming breakthroughs of international importance; breakthroughs that could supposedly alter a business in such a way that a great advantage to the business, but especially the consumer, could be realized.

Little if anything, however, was ever realized from the "inventions" of this second group of individuals, termed "inventors," except the bilking of the public and big-spending investors from industry for almost unimaginable sums of money.

"Inventor" Louis Enricht was one of the latter. But his pronouncement of a cheap substitute for gasoline sounded just like what the doctor ordered for curing an energy crisis. And one had to admit that this enterprising resident of Farmingdale, New York, thought big.

He let it be known in April of 1916 that he had perfected this substitute for gasoline which was a green fluid with an odor of bitter almond. Two ounces of this, when added to two gallons of water, Enricht said, would fuel a car at the ridiculously low price of about one cent per gallon.

This welcome news hit the papers when Europe was at war and the price of gasoline was soaring in this country because fuel was being exported to aid our future allies.

A low-pressure salesman, 70-year-old Enricht allowed a group of goggle-eyed reporters to watch a demonstration at his Farmingdale residence, about thirty miles from Manhattan. The car was inspected by the reporters to make sure that there was no gas in the tank or that a secret tank was not hidden somewhere. Filling a bucket with water from a garden hose, he added his green substance, poured the mixture into the empty gasoline tank, cranked up his car and drove off. Then, acting like a man who had built a better mousetrap, he waited for the world to beat a path to his door. This is exactly what happened, in spite of statements by several prominent scientists that the use of water mixed with anything to fuel an internal combustion engine was impossible.

The first VIP to push the doorbell at Enricht's modest home was William E. Haskell, publisher of the Chicago *Herald.* Like the reporters, Haskell became an instant convert after being given a demonstration and began spreading the cheap-gas gospel. Next, who should appear on Long Island but Henry Ford, who was in New York on other business, including campaigning for the presidency under Republican auspices, but thought it wise to visit Farmingdale. Mr. Ford, too, was greatly impressed after seeing the green liquid and water actually work. The next day, when interviewed by reporters in New York, Ford said that he was interested enough in this project to have ordered a new car sent to Enricht for experimentation and that he expected to have the results of the tests in a week or so.

Meanwhile the newspapers were digging into Enricht's history. On April 28, 1916, it was revealed that he had been involved in several minor swindles including a mail fraud that carried a $500 fine. Who cared? Apparently nobody. Just a week later readers of the financial pages of *The New York Times* blinked at these headlines: MAXIM CO. HAS RIGHT TO NEW MOTOR FUEL. MUNITIONS CORPORATION SAID TO HAVE PAID $1,000,000 TO ENRICHT FOR HIS DISCOVERY. In the Enricht sweepstakes Henry Ford appeared to have been left behind.

The *Times* story told of Maxim's buying land on Long Island for a factory and a laboratory, and described the benefits that the new, cheap fuel would give to America's farmers as well as her motorists. It ended by stating that Enricht, in characteristic fashion, refused to confirm or deny a deal with Maxim. But, the article added, signs of material prosperity around the inventor's home indicated he was obtaining money from somebody. He casually dropped word that he was currently working on a cheap substitute for babbitt metal, an alloy used for bearings, and a process for the extraction of nitrogen from air.

Apparently, someone had spoken out of turn, for the very next day Hudson Maxim, the company's consulting engineer, let some air out of the balloon. He told reporters that the Maxim Company had "only an option on the 'green gasoline' discovery of Louis Enricht and would not buy all rights until the matter was thoroughly investigated . . . I never saw any of this substitute for gasoline . . . why, I have not even met Enricht."

After this letdown, things cooled off and Enricht presumably went back to his experimenting. Toward the end of 1917, with America now at war in Europe, he again made headlines. One of his neighbors, Benjamin F. Yoakum, a prominent railroad financier who, in spite of his Wall Street background, was a trusting soul who had fallen hard for the "green gasoline" story and had gone into business with Enricht, charged that Enricht was selling his valuable secret formula to the Germans. This traitorous plot, Yoakum averred in a complaint filed in court, had been initiated on the German commercial submarine *Deutschland* in Baltimore harbor before America took up arms. Except for having visited the submarine, German-born Enricht denied everything.

167

In the belief that Enricht's magic formula was in a safety deposit box that both he and Enricht had keys to and which could only be opened with both keys, Yoakum obtained a court order to open it. Enricht said the formula was' in his head, that there was nothing in the box but Liberty Bonds, which turned out to be correct. It was Yoakum's turn to join the parade of tycoons with red faces.

Enricht later sold stock in a company formed to extract gasoline from peat which resulted in a grand larceny indictment that, in February of 1923, put him behind the bars of New York's Sing Sing Prison. When Enricht died a few years later, *The Times,* which had found him a source of so much interesting copy during his heyday, failed even to note his passing. With him died the secret of how he was able to fool the reporters, Haskell, Ford, the Maxim Company and his neighbor Yoakum.

Why all the fuss about trying to be the first to cross the Atlantic Ocean in a balloon? Haven't balloonists Malcolm Forbes and Karl Thomas heard that it was done—in 1844—by some Britishers in a craft named the *Victoria*?

Those blokes made it from Wales to Sullivan's Island near Charleston, South Carolina, in a mere 75 hours. A full account of the happening was printed in a New York daily newspaper, the *Sun.* The newspaper dispatch, datelined Charleston, was the brainchild of that master storyteller Edgar Allan Poe, while working as a *Sun* reporter.

It was all a hoax, as readers of the paper soon discovered. The readers were well aware of the idea of balloon travel and had no trouble swallowing Poe's amazing story of a three-day journey across the Atlantic by eight aeronauts.

Here is the final entry in the mythical journal of the flight, written at 1 p.m. on the third day after takeoff.

"We are in full view of the low coast of South Carolina. The great problem is accomplished. We have crossed the Atlantic—fairly and easily crossed it in a balloon! God be praised! Who shall say that anything is impossible hereafter?"

WOODROW WILSON
CONSIDERED STEPPING DOWN

Although Richard Nixon was the first president actually to resign the highest office in the land, there was at least one other who, for different reasons, gave serious thought to making the same decision. Near the end of his first term in 1916, Woodrow Wilson found himself in the midst of a dilemma.

In 1916 the world was in crisis. As huge armies engaged each other on several fronts in Europe, the Kaiser's U-boats were torpedoing enemy warships and neutral merchantmen alike. Although officially proclaiming neutrality, most American sympathies were with the Allies headed by France, England and Russia. The United States and Germany were on a collision course. Within this volatile setting, American voters had to face the polls in November to either give Wilson a second term or replace him with New Yorker Charles Evans Hughes, who had resigned from the Supreme Court to enter the presidential race on the GOP ticket.

Wilson championed peace and progressivism in his presidential campaign of 1916. Although Hughes was himself a moderate progressive, he could not come out in support of a progressive program without endorsing the Democratic record or offending the conservative and business leaders of the Republican party who supported his nomination. Hughes was hard put to openly oppose Wilson's position of neutrality concerning both Europe and Mexico without losing votes. He finally found a plank for his platform in the Adamson Act which included a provision for an eight-hour day for railway workers involved in interstate transportation. Hughes assailed Congress and the President for approving the legislation in response to intimidation from the railway workers who had threatened to strike. *The New York Times* quoted Hughes's statement about the importance of the issue: "Transcending every other issue is the issue that has just presented itself—whether the Government shall yield to force. . . . This country must never know the rule of force. It must never know legislation under oppression."

Wilson, in turn, gained some votes for himself with his interpretation of the Republican position in a speech on September 7 before the Young Men's Democratic League. In response to GOP attacks upon his foreign policy, Wilson made the assumption that this attack implied the Republicans meant to change foreign policy if they won the election. The New York *World* reported his speech which included the following:

There is only one choice as against peace, and that is war. Some of the supporters of that party (the Republican), a very great body of the supporters of that party, outspokenly declare that they want war; so that the certain prospect of the success of the Republican Party is that we shall be drawn in one form or other into the embroilments of the European war, and that to the south of us the force of the United States will be used to produce in Mexico the kind of law and order which some American investors in Mexico consider most to their advantage.

Extremely concerned not only about the outcome of the election but also about the welfare of the nation, Wilson made an unprecedented move. On the day before the election he wrote an extraordinary letter to his Secretary of State, Robert Lansing, which included the following:

Again and again the question has arisen in my mind, What would it be my duty to do were Mr. Huges to be elected? Four months would elapse before he could take charge of the affairs of the government, and during those four months I would be without such moral backing from the nation as would be necessary to steady and control our relations with other governments. I would be known to be the rejected, not the accredited, spokesman of the country; and yet the accredited spokesman would be without legal authority to speak for the nation. Such a situation would be fraught with the gravest dangers. The direction of the foreign policy of the government would in effect have been taken out of my hands and yet its new definition would be impossible until March.

I feel it would be my duty to relieve the country of the perils of such a situation at once. The course I have in mind is dependent upon the consent and cooperation of the Vice President; but, if I could gain his consent to the plan, I would ask your permission to invite Mr. Hughes to become Secretary of State and would then join the Vice President in resigning, and thus open to Mr. Hughes the immediate succession to the presidency.

At the time, the Presidential Succession Act of 1886 had not been amended to put an elected official, the Speaker of the House of Representatives, at the top of the succession list after the Vice President. Hence, in 1916, if Wilson and his Vice President, Thomas Riley Marshall, had vacated their offices, the Secretary of State would have moved into the White House.

Although Wilson won the election, it was days before he could be certain there was no need to actualize his unique proposal for a smooth transferral of the presidential office. On election night, early returns from the East showed Hughes so far ahead that the newspapers issued "Extras" announcing a Republican victory; and ebullient ex-President Theodore Roosevelt issued a statement: "I am doubly thankful as an American for the election of Mr. Hughes. It is a vindication of our national honor."

The next morning the papers admitted that the election was in doubt, and it soon became apparent that the outcome depended on how California voted. By November 9, two days after the balloting, Wilson was confident enough to leave Washington for a trip on the presidential yacht *Mayflower*. But not until November 22, after every last California vote had been tallied and double-checked did Charles Evans Hughes send congratulations to his victorious opponent.

In response to numerous other criticisms of the lame duck period between election in November and inauguration in March, the 20th Amendment to the Constitution was ratified in 1933. This "Lame Duck Amendment" provided that the term of office of the President and the Vice President would begin on January 20, more than six weeks closer to the election.

Salt Lake City · Provo · Price · Green River · Vernal · Watson · Mack · *UTAH* · *COLO.*

BANK BY MAIL

Should your travels ever take you through the town of Vernal, Utah, on U.S. 40 thirty miles west of the Colorado line, stop for a moment on Main Street for a look at the building with the sign ZION'S FIRST NATIONAL BANK. There probably is no other building like it anywhere, not because of its appearance or because of the amount of money in its vault, but because 80,000 of the textured bricks on the face of the bank came all the way from Salt Lake City by mail.

From 1903 to 1917 Vernal had a small bank of the usual frontier type, with a steel-lined counter surrounded by a bullet-proof screen as protection against holdups. But with the town growing as a trading center for farmers, cattlemen, sheepherders and miners, it wasn't long before a larger bank was needed. A man named William P. Coltharp planned a large building, to be constructed on Main Street, that would include roomy quarters for the bank. The architect from Salt Lake City who designed the

172

Coltharp Mercantile Company building project felt that while homemade red brick would be good enough for the inside walls, the building should be faced with textured brick made by the Pressed Brick Company of Salt Lake City.

Vernal is only 125 miles from Salt Lake City as the crow flies. But there was, and still is, no railroad between Vernal and Salt Lake City, and in those days no highway worthy of the name connecting the two places. The bricks could have been brought by wagon over a rough trail but the cost seemed prohibitive—several times what the bricks were worth. So a cheaper way was sought.

Just who discovered the solution is not a matter of record. Some say it was the bank's cashier and in later years its president, the late Nicholas J. Meagher. But whoever it was, he or she made the interesting discovery that parcel post rates for their area were based on circles drawn with Salt Lake City as their center. Regardless of what route a package had to take to get there, Vernal fell within a circle with a radius of less than 175 miles and therefore could take advantage of a very favorable rate. So the Pressed Brick Company received its orders: Pack 80,000 textured bricks in 50-pound packages, address them to the bank, and mail them from the Salt Lake City Post Office.

In order to reach Vernal, only 125 miles away, the 50-pound shipments, like any other mail from Salt Lake City, actually had to go nearly 400 miles. At Salt Lake City they were put aboard the Denver & Rio Grande Western Railroad for a 265-mile ride south and east through Provo, Price, and Green River, Utah, to Mack, Colorado, just west of Grand Junction. At Mack they were transferred to a now defunct narrow-gauge line running in a generally northerly direction around mountains and back over the Colorado-Utah boundary to a tiny Utah community called Watson— about 60 miles. At Watson it was onto freight wagons for the last leg of the journey—another 65 or so miles—which included a ferry crossing of Green River southeast of Vernal. The wagon trip required four days each way. Two wagons traveled together so that the two teams could be doubled up when necessary on unusually steep grades.

For a while everything went smoothly. Then the bricks began to back up in the Mack Post Office. A worried postmaster in Salt Lake City wired for advice to the Postmaster General in Washington, D.C. Hurried conferences resulted in a new regulation limiting to 200 pounds the weight that a sender could ship to any one consignee in a day. It made little difference. Tons and tons of bricks were already en route. The new regulation was side-stepped neatly by having the brick company address the 50-pound shipments to nearby ranchers and residents all over Vernal. The consignees picked them up and lugged them to the construction site. Everybody wanted a new bank, and they got it, built just the way the architect had specified.

The Utah volume of the Federal Writers Guide series, published in 1941, states that as a result of the bricks-by-mail episode the farmers in the Vernal area became parcel post happy. They not only began ordering all sorts of things they had never thought of bringing in by mail before, but they began mailing their crops to market: "One shipment of corn required 10 four-ton trucks. Mail trucks were often loaded to capacity without carrying a single letter."

The Federal Writers Guide describes what the postal authorities did to stop the crop shipments through the mails with the simple statement that, "Federal parcel post regulations were changed shortly thereafter."

This is a song to celebrate banks,
Because they are full of money and you go into them
    and all you hear is clinks and clanks,
Or maybe a sound like the wind in the trees on the hills,
Which is the rustling of the thousand-dollar bills.
Most bankers dwell in marble halls,
Which they get to dwell in because they encourage
    deposits and discourage withdralls,
And particularly because they all observe one rule which
    woe betides the banker who fails to heed it,
Which is you must never lend any money to anybody
    unless they don't need it. . .

From *Bankers Are Just Like Anybody Else, Except Richer*, by Ogden Nash

RETURN OF
THE TEXAS LONGHORN

Early in the spring we round up the dogies,
Mark 'em and brand 'em and bob off their tails,
Round up the horses, load up the chuck wagon,
And throw the dogies out on the long trail.

This stanza from a very old song describes in a few lines a way of life for thousands of Texans during the great trail driving era of a century ago. Life for the cowboys on the trail revolved around the famous Texas longhorns for, come good weather or bad, the beef herds on which they all depended for a living had to be continually pushed northward to Kansas railheads for shipment to market. The longhorns were descendants of cattle brought to North America by Spanish explorers and for some twenty years after the Civil War, these rangy critters with their long legs and widely-flaring, needle-pointed horns were the life blood of the Lone Star State.

175

But having served their purpose, the longhorns eventually were replaced by other breeds and virtually disappeared. Fortunately, thanks to the efforts in the late 1920's of a handful of nostalgic Southwesterners, the longhorns were rescued from extinction and are today enjoying some of the fame garnered in earlier days by the hardy members of their race who once plodded by the millions up the historic cattle trails of the old West.

Texas stockmen returning home from the Civil War had found the grazing areas of their state overrun by half-wild longhorns. As barbwire had not yet been invented, the animals had ranged wherever they could find pasturage. With most of the able-bodied men in the Confederate army for four years and nobody on hand to interfere with the longhorn's breeding habits, they had proliferated amazingly. They numbered nearly three and a half million, a generally accepted estimate.

With all this beef available, and the populous East clamoring for it, one might think the Texas cattlemen could quickly have restored a measure of prosperity to their war-ravaged economy. But there was no way to hook up the supply with the demand because the Texas cattle country was not yet served by railroads. Old overland trails to eastern Kansas and central Missouri were used by drovers before the war but had closed down as homesteaders and farmers moved in and took possession of vacant land. Those millions of rangy longhorns had no place to go, and as long as they stayed in Texas they were worth almost nothing.

While longhorn meat may not have been the tenderest in the world, the big, ungainly, ill-tempered animal that came in an astonishing variety of colors and markings had other characteristics that were admirable under the right circumstances. The longhorn could travel great distances without water. Because it had long ago become accustomed to shifting for itself, it could rustle grub where other breeds would starve. The longhorn could take the heat of the merciless prairie sun. All of this suddenly became important when an enterprising 29-year-old Illinois cattle dealer, Joseph G. McCoy, came up with a possible solution to the Texans' problem of how to link the meat supply with the demand.

McCoy had heard all about these Texas longhorns from another Illinois cattle dealer, William Sugg, who in 1866 had purchased a large herd in Texas and attempted to drive it to Sedalia, Missouri. The results had been disastrous as farmers refused to let him and other drovers pass over their land. McCoy also knew that a new railroad, the Kansas Pacific, was inching westward from Kansas City toward the Rockies.

With the daring that characterized the entrepreneurs of his time, he decided to install shipping pens at a likely spot beside the newly laid rails and invited Texas ranchers to drive their herds overland to the market he was establishing there. The young promoter needed a spot that the tide of western agrarian immigration had not yet reached. In other words, it had to be in virtually uninhabited country or the farmers would be out with their shotguns and pitchforks to block the new cattle trails. He needed a spot with plenty of water to slake the thirst of the steers and cow ponies that had walked hundreds of miles. He also needed limitless prairie grass for grazing the herds that would have to be held in the vicinity in case the demand for cattle cars temporarily exceeded the supply. The place he picked was Abilene, Kansas.

In the early summer of 1867 Abilene consisted of a dozen or so log houses and stores close to the Smoky Hill River, about one hundred miles directly west of Topeka. The change in sleepy little Abilene was rapid. In McCoy's own words, "In sixty days from July 1st a shipping yard that would accommodate three thousand cattle, a large pair of Fairbank's scales, a barn and office were completed, and a good three-story hotel on the way to completion."

Almost as soon as the first plank had been nailed on his cattle pens, McCoy had sent his friend Sugg riding southward to intercept desperate Texas drovers that rumor said were moving northward through the Indian Nation (now Oklahoma) with herds for which they somehow hoped to find a market. Rather amazingly, it all worked. Longhorns arrived, McCoy had a buyer for them and on

September 5, 1867, the first trainload of live beef pulled away from McCoy's siding bound for Chicago. With the twenty-car train a new era in the history of America's cattle industry had begun.

To help McCoy celebrate the great event a party of Illinois stockmen came from Springfield. The fact that the new hotel, which McCoy named The Drovers' Cottage, was not completed, failed to put a damper on the affair. McCoy described the party in his book *Cattle Trade of the West and Southwest* published seven years later.

Arriving at Abilene in the evening, several large tents, including one for dining purposes, were found ready for the reception of guests. A substantial repast was spread before the excursionists and devoured with a relish peculiar to camp life, after which wine, toasts, and speechifying were the order until a late hour at night.

Before the sun had mounted high in the heavens on the following day, the iron horse was darting down the Kaw Valley with the first trainload of cattle that ever passed over the Kansas Pacific Railroad, the precursor of many thousands to follow.

According to McCoy's published figures, 35,000 longhorns came bawling into Abilene that first season, enough to fill nearly a thousand cattle cars.

During the following winter McCoy publicized his new venture throughout Texas. At the same time, since buyers were as important as sellers, he advertised in newspapers read by Northern cattle dealers, inviting them to take advantage of the opportunities afforded by Abilene's facilities. What was in all this for McCoy? He had arranged with the Kansas Pacific to pay him a percentage on every carload of longhorns that left his cattle pens. He also owned The Drovers' Cottage, which offered soft beds to trail drivers who had been sleeping on the hard ground for weeks.

In the summer of 1868 seventy-five thousand Texas longhorns plodded north to Abilene, most of them following the route running almost directly north from Fort Worth that would become famous in song and story as the

Chisholm Trail.[1] The next year that number doubled.

With trail crews riding in all summer, with their herds often numbering two thousand head, Abilene was growing and prospering. But farmers, too, were coming into the region, and they objected to having their fences and crops trampled. Moreover, the town's permanent residents grew tired of the vice and gunplay that prevailed with the annual influx of the wild Texas cowboys. In 1872 the trail drivers were officially notified that the welcome mat at Abilene had been worn out. Joseph McCoy took what he could get for his holdings and moved to Wichita. This Kansas town was quick to take advantage of Abilene's abdication and the bonanza created by what was now a veritable flood of longhorn cattle moving north from Texas every summer. The riches and notoriety were shared by the towns of Ellsworth and Newton, later by Caldwell and Dodge City. The last-named became the busiest and wickedest cow town of them all.

For more than a dozen years after Abilene went back to being just another sleepy little prairie town, the hardy longhorns kept coming up the various well-defined trails to Kansas and Nebraska to be shipped by rail to Northern markets or to continue on to Wyoming and Montana for stocking the ranges there. After most of the buffalo were killed off by white hide hunters, longhorns were driven north to feed Uncle Sam's wards on Indian reservations. The adventures of one such herd are described in that famous narrative of trail-driving days, *The Log of a Cowboy* by Andy Adams. The old song summed it up this way:

> Oh, you'll be soup for Uncle Sam's Injuns;
> It's "Beef, heap beef," you hear 'em cry;
> Git along, git along, git along, little dogies,
> For the Injuns they'll eat you by-and-by.

But the westward surge of homesteading farmers, with their sod-breaking plows and barbwire fences, along with

[1] For a story about this trail, see *The Old Chisholm Trail* on page 88.

the building of railroads into central Texas, eventually wrote the end to the era of the great trail drives and the heyday of the old-time American cowboy. As the drives ended, so did the usefulness of the historic Texas longhorn.

With the longhorn's ability to withstand the rigors of the cattle trail no longer of importance, the famous animal soon was replaced by stodgier breeds of cattle, unromantic bovines to be sure, but producers of better beef and more of it. The rangy animal became a museum piece, with his unique head ornaments often measuring five or six feet in a straight line from tip to tip, mounted and hung over ranch house fireplaces or behind the bars of saloons for Eastern visitors to wonder at. Like the buffalo, the longhorn came close to extinction.

There were many who had interesting, if not fond, memories of the cantankerous beast that had made many a bankrupt Texan solvent again. But nobody did anything about a rescue operation until it was almost too late. Fortunately a small group of former cattlemen in the U.S. Forest Service decided that the Southwest really owed the longhorn more than just a memorial plaque in a museum.

In 1927, sixty-nine-year-old Will Barnes, onetime Arizona rancher and author of numerous books and articles on the West, headed the Save-the-Longhorn crusade. With the help of Texas-born Senator John B. Kendrick of Wyoming, he talked Congress into appropriating $3,000 for the purpose of buying a small breeding herd and placing it on a government reservation, provided, of course, that suitable specimens could be found. Even Barnes wasn't sure he could bring it off. Such longhorns as remained running wild in the thickets of Texas probably had been contaminated by the Brahman and other strains.

But Barnes and another Forest Service man, John H. Hatton, set out on their search. Among the Texas stockmen whose aid they enlisted was Graves Peeler of Jourdanton, who was working as a range detective for the Texas & Southwestern Cattle Raisers' Association. Peeler's travels and background had given him a vast knowledge of the state's cattle population which proved indispensable. Barnes and Hatton crisscrossed Texas and even went into

Mexico following leads, sometimes mere rumors, of good longhorn specimens. Barnes recorded their experiences for the October 15, 1927, issue of *The Saturday Evening Post.* Here is his summary of the results, modestly put in the third person.

In their search for genuine specimens the men traveled almost 5,000 miles over the grassy plains and through the mesquite thickets of southern Texas. They searched through the dry *resacas* along the Rio Grande and looked through miles of cottonwood *bosques* for what they sought. They rode miles through dense forests of mesquite or thickets of prickly pear, cat's claw and huisache, where every limb was decorated with fishhook thorns or needle-like spines of cactus. They looked through thousands and thousands of cattle in pastures, in round-ups, stockyards and open fields often 20,000 to 30,000 acres in extent. From them all they selected the twenty-three animals they deemed worthy of being classed as true types of the historic old Longhorn cattle.

Barnes and Hatton had rounded up ten cows and two bulls in the coastal area between Beaumont and Corpus Christi and ten more cows and another bull in the thickets of southwest Texas. Three steers were also brought along for exhibition purposes when the breeding herd was shipped to the Wichita Mountains Wildlife Refuge near Cache, Oklahoma. The steer is the member of the breed that produces those prize-winning horns. Perhaps this achievement is his way of compensating for his involuntary celibacy.

So the longhorn had been saved. This was all very fine, but the longhorn was a product of Texas and to certain old-timers there the longhorn seemed a bit out of place in Oklahoma. Hence it was not long before J. Frank Dobie, author and folklorist of note, was knocking on Graves Peeler's door and asking what the chances were for rounding up a few more longhorns for the honor of the Lone Star State. Dobie said that Fort Worth oilman Sid Richardson would pay the bill this time. The result was another search through thickets and pastures. About half

181

the specimens collected formed the foundation herd for the hundred or so longhorns that may be seen today in seven Texas state parks. Graves Peeler became so intrigued by the animals that he kept the other half and started his own private longhorn herd on his ranch in McMullen County.

About three hundred longhorns, descendants of the original twenty-three brought to the Oklahoma refuge by Barnes and Hatton, are on exhibition there today. A slightly smaller herd, started in 1938 with progeny of the first, enjoys life at Fort Niobrara Wildlife Refuge near Valentine, Nebraska. As both herds must be kept down to the capacity of the available pasturage, excess animals are auctioned off periodically, usually in the fall. Buyers are chiefly Southwestern cattlemen, many of them members of the Texas Longhorn Breeders Association which was formed in 1964 to establish longhorn standards and serve as a medium of communication between the constantly growing number of longhorn owners.

Not only are today's cattlemen interested in having members of the historic breed around their ranches to remind them of the exciting past, but also to carry on experiments designed to utilize the longhorn's best qualities in crossbreeding with conventional cattle. The roster of active members of the Association is about one hundred and seventy-five. While most are in the West and South, the list includes breeders as far north as Wisconsin and Ontario and as far east as Massachusetts.

One of the largest private longhorn herds—about five hundred head—is owned by Walter B. Scott of Goliad, Texas, a past president of the Association. Rancher Scott's cattle, wearing a wineglass brand, graze in lush pastures not far from what was once the main stem of the Chisholm Trail, best known of all the old cattle trails and one whose history may well have been on the mind of the unknown cowboy poet who more than eighty years ago penned this chorus:

> Whoopee ti yi yo, git along, little dogies;
> It's your misfortune and none of my own.
> Whoopee ti yi yo, git along, little dogies;
> For old Wyoming will be your new home.

ONE WAY TO
SHARE THE WEALTH

A starry-eyed investor who puts his money behind a Broadway play is often referred to as an "angel" by theater people. "Archangel" would better describe Texas oil tycoon Edgar Davis, who spent well over a million dollars on actors' salaries and theater rental to keep his pet play running in New York City. This he did for more than two years despite harsh words from the critics and almost complete disinterest on the part of the playgoing public.

The Ladder, written by newspaperman J. Frank Davis, an old friend and admirer of, although no relation to, the play's financial backer, was concerned with reincarnation. The action extended for over 600 years, beginning in the year 1300 in an English castle. The same characters were then put in the setting of London in 1679, then New York City of 1844 and finally New York City of 1926, the year the play opened to a puzzled audience. The program explained that the title for the play, *The Ladder,* came from a poem, *Gradatim,* written by Josiah Gilbert Holland:

> Heaven is not reached at a single bound
> But we build the ladder by which we rise
> From the lowly earth to the vaulted skies,
> And we mount to its summit round by round.

Broadway critics were most unkind to *The Ladder.* Alexander Woollcott called it "a large, richly upholstered piece of nothing at all." Brooks Atkinson complimented the scenery, the costumes and the leading lady. But, as far as the acting was concerned, he dismissed it with a line from the famed British literary critic Samuel Johnson: "Declamation roar'd, while Passion slept."

But "Archangel" Davis was not an easily discouraged man. At a comparatively young age he had made a fortune in the rubber industry in Sumatra. On his arrival in the Texas oil fields in the early 1920's, he spent his fortune having six wells drilled and all were dry holes. Then with borrowed money, he drilled a seventh which was a gusher. In 1926 he sold his oil interests to the Magnolia Petroleum Company for $12,000,000 and embarked on a career of philanthropy, which included endowing charitable foundations at Luling, Texas, and Brockton, Massachusetts, as well as backing *The Ladder.*

As far as the critics and the public were concerned, *The Ladder* was just another dry hole. But Davis refused to close the play regardless of the cost. After the show had played to small audiences for two months, he made the entire house free for the performance on Christmas Day, 1926. The following April he announced that admission would be refunded to any dissatisfied patron attending the play. At the same time, he started offering $500 weekly prizes for the best essays on *The Ladder.* Beginning in November of 1927, tickets to the show were handed out free to all comers, a move that received considerable publicity but still failed to pack the house. Seven months later admission charges were reinstated.

By August of 1928, Davis was showing signs that he had

had about enough. He ran quarter-page advertisements in the New York City newspapers headed "The Truth About The Ladder" and explaining his philosophy of life. The ad concluded with this warning: "If The Ladder, in substantially its present form at the Cort Theater, does not give evidence of being self-sustaining by about November 1, it will be withdrawn."

The play continued to be a flop and Davis, true to his word, closed it on a Saturday night in November, a little more than two years after it first opened on Broadway. But there was another surprise coming. Over the weekend, Davis moved *The Ladder* to Boston, with all seats at a dollar and a money-back guarantee if you failed to enjoy the show. Tickets soon became free here, as they had in New York City. Concerning a Boston performance, authors Abel Green and Joe Laurie, Jr. wrote in their book *Show Biz:* "Admission was for the asking, and as is axiomatic when anything is 'for free,' few came. You could arrest the ticket taker and the box office man for vagrancy. We were in an audience comprising ten other people, all sur-le-cuff."

Theater lore is replete with critical wit. One reviewer, furious at having to suffer through a particularly bad performance of *King Lear*, had but one comment: "Mr. Clarke played the King all evening as though under constant fear that someone else was about to play the Ace."

The late Charles Frohman, on the other hand, was likely to sum up plays most felicitously in telegrams. Once, when he was producing an English comedy at his cherished Empire Theater in New York, he received just after the première a cable of eager, though decently nervous, inquiry from the author in London, who could not bear to wait until the reviews and the box-office statements reached him. "How's it going?" was the inquiry. Frohman cabled back: "It's gone."

From "Capsule Criticism," by Alexander Woollcott

**Roosevelt to Move Thanksgiving;
Retailers for It, Plymouth Is N**

Football Schedule Makers
Headache, With Sea
With Fifth Thursd

By The Associated Press
CAMPOBELLO ISLAND, N. ?
Aug. 14.—President Roosevelt
nounced today that he was sha'
ing another precedent and mo
up the date of Thanksgiving
year from Nov. 30 to Nov. 23.
Explaining his decision during
informal press conference at
boyhood Summer cottage here, t
President said that in the last si
years many persons, most of them
retailers, had urged him to shift the
annual feast day from the tradi-
tional last Thursday of November
to some earlier date. They had contended that Thanksgiving Day
came too close to Christmas and
was no break between

WHEN TURKEY DAY WAS TWINS

Ever since Philadelphia's Sara Josepha Hale, editor of *Godey's Lady's Book* and author of "Mary Had a Little Lamb," persuaded Abraham Lincoln to proclaim a national Thanksgiving Day, the time-honored holiday featuring stuffed turkey, cranberries, and pumpkin pie had been observed on the last Thursday of November. But seventy-five years of tradition did not bother Franklin D. Roosevelt when he thought tradition should accede to practicable profit.

On August 14, 1939, the President announced that since the coming Thanksgiving happened to fall on November 30, which left only three weeks and two days for the country's annual Christmas shopping spree, he was moving Turkey Day forward by a week. This would generate more business for the retail stores, and there would be a longer period of temporary work in the stores for jobless people. This made economic sense to him, as the country was still in the midst of the Depression.

Many people were upset by this announcement, particularly those concerned with the national fall preoccupation known as football. Most colleges and even high schools had scheduled the big game of the season for Thursday, November 30. Just how, the coaches wanted to know, could they fill their stadiums on November 30 if it was to be just an ordinary working day?

Roosevelt was also chastised by Massachusetts, where the first Thanksgiving had been celebrated in 1621 in Plymouth. The Board of Selectmen of Plymouth fired off a blistering letter to the President, while its chairman, James Frazier, announced that the Pilgrim capital would stand fast against all such tampering with the celebrated day. "It is a religious holiday," Frazier declared, "and the President has no right to change it for commercial interests."

One Republican senator suggested that perhaps the Chief Executive would like to break another precedent and abolish winter.

Actually, each governor had the power to pick his own date for Thanksgiving for the President's selection was binding only on the District of Columbia and the territories of the United States. However, since governors are politicians, a poll showed that most Democrats would play "Follow the Leader" and accept the new date, whereas Republican governors considered it a partisan issue and wanted no part of it. The Texas governor stood out with the unique solution of celebrating both holidays.

Amid all the uproar, the people who supplied Thanksgiving dinner's main course were unperturbed. The turkey growers didn't seem to care one way or the other. With sufficient advance notice, they said, it was just as easy to fatten a bird for one day as another.

When the new Thanksgiving arrived on November 23, America was about evenly divided. Citizens of twenty-three states, including all of New England, were going about their usual business and looking forward to giving thanks and feasting according to the date on their calendars—November 30. Twenty-two states were in the Roosevelt camp due to the President's persuasiveness and popularity rather than to their own inclinations. Colorado and Mississippi followed the example of Texas and contented themselves with a double holiday.

In 1940, the year Roosevelt broke with another tradition and ran for a third term, he put on a repeat performance of the Thanksgiving Day switch. The following May the President announced that he was committed to moving Thanksgiving forward again. At the same time, however, he conceded that he had been wrong about the expected boost in retail trade envisaged when he first shifted the holiday. Department of Commerce figures indicated, he admitted, that nothing had been gained business-wise, and much ado had been made about what had appeared to be nothing. Therefore, he concluded, with a twinkle in his eye, starting in 1942 the country could go back to its old habit of observing the holiday on the last Thursday of November.

However, in December of 1941, Congress, in order to make sure of the President's intentions, asserted itself and passed a resolution fixing forever the fourth Thursday of November as Thanksgiving Day. The good people of Massachusetts, governors, Congress, football coaches and calendar printers breathed a sigh of relief as FDR affixed his signature to the document.

Virginia historians for many years contended that the first Thanksgiving in the New World was held at Berkeley Plantation in 1619, two years before the Pilgrim observance.

In reply to protests that Virginia was not mentioned in President Kennedy's Thanksgiving Proclamation of 1962 came this message: "The President has asked me to reply to your telegram about the Thanksgiving Proclamation statement. You are quite right, and I can only plead an unconquerable New England bias on the part of the White House staff.

"We are all grateful to you for reminding us of the Berkeley Hundred Thanksgiving, and I can assure you that the error will not be repeated in the future."

The next year President Kennedy's Proclamation began: "Over three centuries ago, our forefathers in Virginia and in Massachusetts, far from home in a lonely wilderness, set aside a time for thanksgiving. . ."

ABOUT THE AUTHOR

John I. White's interest in Americana dates from 1924, when, after graduation from the University of Maryland, he spent the summer in Arizona and became intrigued by the ballads of the old West.

In the fall of 1926, after working a year and a half on the Washington *Star,* he moved to New York to attend Columbia Graduate School. Radio was in its infancy at the time. John managed to get an audition with NBC and was soon strumming a guitar and singing on the air for fifteen minutes one afternoon a week just for fun. After a few months he switched to WOR, where he was paid for doing the same thing. Concurrently, he took a "summer" job in New York with a publishing firm which lasted for thirty-eight years. The radio work continued for ten years, and the last five were with an NBC network show "Death Valley Days." There was also time for recording twenty songs for the American Record Corporation, most of them released under pseudonyms—Whitey Johns, Jimmie Price, The Lone Star Ranger and The Lonesome Cowboy.

Upon retirement from business eleven years ago, John was able to combine two avocations into a full-time effort—research and writing on American history, particularly the West, and writing about the songs he used to sing on the air.

His latest magazine work (of some 40-odd) is a ten-page article on Nebraska's sod houses in the March, 1975 issue of *The American West.*

An anthology of his published works on old Western songs, plus new material, titled *Git Along, Little Dogies,* was issued by University of Illinois Press in 1975.

Original illustrations on pages 9, 12, 17, 27, 41, 43, 46, 56, 63, 73, 81, 88, 92, 99, 106, 111, 118, 147, 151, 165, 172, 175, 183, 186 by Jerry Allison.

ACKNOWLEDGMENTS

Grateful acknowledgment is made to the following for permission to reprint selections included in this book:

Doubleday & Co., Inc. for a selection from *Lafayette: A Life* by Andreas Latzko, copyright 1936 by Andreas Latzko.

Research Reprints, Inc. for a selection from *Lafayette in America* by A. Levasseur, reprinted 1970 by Research Reprints, Inc.

Dover Publications, Inc. for a selection from *The Octagon House* by Orson S. Fowler, copyright 1973 by Dover Publications, Inc.

Hawthorn Books, Inc. for a selection from *Niagara Country* by Lloyd Graham, copyright 1949 by Lloyd Graham.

University of Washington Press for a selection from *Mercer's Belles* by Roger Conant, copyright 1960 by the University of Washington Press.

American History Illustrated for "Alaska Puzzle" by John I. White, from the June, 1967 issue, copyright 1967 by Historical Times, Inc.

Macmillan Publishing Co., Inc. for a selection from *The Old-Time Cowhand* by Ramon F. Adams, copyright 1948, 1949, 1951, 1954, 1959, 1960, 1961 by Ramon F. Adams.

Interland Publishing Inc. for a selection from *The Grand Duke Alexis in the United States of America,* copyright 1972 by Interland Publishing Inc.

Frances Jacobs Alberts for a selection from *Sod House Memories, Volume II* by Frances Jacobs Alberts, copyright 1967 by Frances Jacobs Alberts.

Purcells, Inc. for a selection from *Sod Walls* by Roger L. Welsch, copyright 1968 by Purcells, Inc.

Harper & Row, Publishers, Inc. for a selection from *Mark Twain's Autobiography* by Samuel Langhorne Clemens, copyright 1924 by Clara Gabrilowitsch.

Yankee for "Henry Blew the Whistle" by John I. White, from the May, 1971 issue, published by Yankee, Inc., copyright 1971 by Yankee, Inc.

Wayne State University Press for a selection from *Monopoly on Wheels* by William Greenleaf, copyright 1961 by Wayne State University Press.

Harper & Row, Publishers, Inc. for a selection from *Horseless Carriage Days* by Hiram Percy Maxim, copyright 1936, 1937 by Harper & Brothers.

FOR FURTHER READING

Living Laboratory
  Richard Dunlop, *Doctors of the American Frontier*, Doubleday & Company, Inc., 1965.

Happiness Was An Octagon
  Orson S. Fowler, *The Octagon House*, Dover Publications, Inc., 1973. Reprint of 1853 edition.

A Remarkable Little Lady
  Charles Neilson Gattey, *The Bloomer Girls*, Coward-McCann, Inc., 1967.

Lincoln Wanted Only One War
  Bruce Catton, *Terrible Swift Sword*, Doubleday & Company, Inc., 1963.

Mission from Muscovy
  Alexandre Tarsaidze, *Czars and Presidents*, McDowell, Obolensky Inc., 1958.

Confederates South of the Border
  Andrew F. Rolle, *The Lost Cause: The Confederate Exodus to Mexico*, The University of Oklahoma Press, 1965.

The Collins Overland Telegraph
  Perry McDonough Collins, *Siberian Journey: Down the Amur to the Pacific 1856-1857*, University of Wisconsin Press, 1962.

Brides for Seattle
  Roger Conant; edited by Lenna Deutsch, *Mercer's Belles: The Journal of a Reporter*, University of Washington Press, 1960.

Alaska Puzzle
  Hector Chevigny, *Russian America*, Viking Press, 1965.

Strangers in Pharoah-Land
  William B. Hesseltine and Hazel C. Wolf, *The Blue and Gray on the Nile*, University of Chicago Press, 1961.

Henry Blew the Whistle
  William Greenleaf, *Monopoly on Wheels*, Wayne State University Press, 1961.
  Hiram Percy Maxim, *Horseless Carriage Days*, Harper & Brothers, 1936 or Dover Publications, Inc., 1962.

How Not to Make a Lake
  George Kennan, *E. H. Harriman, A Biography, Vol. II*, Houghton Mifflin Company, 1922.

Return of the Texas Longhorn
  J. Frank Dobie, *The Longhorns*, Little, Brown & Co., 1941 or paperback by Grossett & Dunlap, 1957.